Creating Effective JavaHelp™

THE JAVA™ SERIES

Learning Java™

Java™ Threads

Java™ Network Programming

Java™ Virtual Machine

Java™ AWT Reference

Java™ Language Reference

Java™ Fundamental Classes Reference

Database Programming with JDBC™ and Java™

Java™ Distributed Computing

Developing Java Beans™

Java™ Security

Java™ Cryptography

Java™ Swing

Java™ Servlet Programming

Java™ I/O

Java™ 2D Graphics

Enterprise JavaBeans™

Creating Effective JavaHelp™

Java™ and XML

Also from O'Reilly

Java™ in a Nutshell

Java™ Examples in a Nutshell

Java™ Enterprise in a Nutshell

Java™ Foundation Classes in a Nutshell

Java™ Power Reference: A Complete Searchable
   Resource on CD-ROM

Creating Effective JavaHelp™

Kevin Lewis

O'REILLY®

Beijing · Cambridge · Farnham · Köln · Paris · Sebastopol · Taipei · Tokyo

Creating Effective JavaHelp™
by Kevin Lewis

Copyright © 2000 O'Reilly & Associates, Inc. All rights reserved.
Printed in the United States of America.

Published by O'Reilly & Associates, Inc., 101 Morris Street, Sebastopol, CA 95472.

Editors: John Posner and Mike Loukides

Production Editor: Mary Anne Weeks Mayo

Cover Designer: Hanna Dyer

Printing History:

      May 2000:   First Edition.

Library of Congress Cataloging-in-Publication Data

Lewis, Kevin
   Creating effective Java help/Kevin Lewis.
     p. cm. -- (The Java series)
   ISBN 1-56592-719-2
   1. Java (Compuer program language) I. Title. II. Series.

QA76.73.J38 L495 2000
005.13'3--dc21   00-32664

ISBN: 1-56592-719-2
[M]   [9/00]

Table of Contents

Preface

This book is about JavaHelp™ from Sun Microsystems. JavaHelp is an online help system developed for the Java™ programming language. It is similar to other help systems, such as WinHelp and HTML Help, in that you use a table of contents (TOC), index, or word-search index to find and display help topics. JavaHelp can be used for many online documentation purposes, but its primary function is to provide an online help system to support Java applications.

Of course, as with any new online help system, people have many questions they need answered and demands they need addressed. This book attempts to address those questions and demands and teaches you how to develop usable online help systems with JavaHelp. To provide a comprehensive look at JavaHelp development, this book covers the main features and options of JavaHelp by presenting the following topics:

- Understanding JavaHelp
- Creating your first HelpSet
- Planning the JavaHelp project
- Preparing help topics
- Creating HelpSet data and navigation files
- Enhancing the HelpSet
- Using the JavaHelp API for advanced presentation options
- Deploying the help system to your users
- Using third-party, help-authoring tools

Audience

While it would probably suffice to say that this book is for any person interested in learning JavaHelp and developing usable JavaHelp systems, I can think of two specific groups of people who will likely get the most out of this book: Java developers and technical writers.

Many Java developers don't have technical writers to handle software documentation. If you are one of these developers, you will find this book a great supplement to your other O'Reilly Java books. You might not have the need or desire to read the book cover to cover (although I recommend you do), but you will find that specific sections give you the information you need. You will want to read at least this Preface and Chapter 1, *Understanding JavaHelp*, to learn how to create a basic JavaHelp system. You should also scan the book for tips on making your help system usable.

The book is also designed for technical writers, who are faced with the challenge of learning many types of documentation systems. As more applications are developed in the Java programming language, you will find a strong need to learn the JavaHelp system. This book will help you learn to develop JavaHelp systems quickly and easily. If you need to master online help systems, you will probably want to read the book cover to cover. However, if you are experienced with online help design and authoring, I have clearly identified sections so that you will know when you can skip over material.

About This Book

This book covers the main features and options of JavaHelp. It presents concepts, chapter by chapter, until you have a complete understanding of how to create usable JavaHelp systems and how to integrate them into applications and Java applets. The key phrase here is *create usable JavaHelp systems*. I emphasize this phrase because this book not only teaches you how to create JavaHelp systems but also provides tips for making those systems usable. If you are an experienced help author, you may not need this extra information. But if you are creating a help system for the first time, you may find that the help-authoring tips are quite helpful. Use them and your application users will be thankful.

Now that you know what this book is about, I should explain what this book is not about. This book is not a manual that focuses on the technical aspects of the JavaHelp application programming interface (API). In fact, you won't find a lot of low-level technical information about JavaHelp in this book. I do cover enough technical information to help you understand how JavaHelp works, and I provide code samples to help you understand how to deploy JavaHelp with your applications. However, the book's focus is primarily on how to work with JavaHelp and how to design and create usable JavaHelp online help systems. If you are interested in learning more about lower-level technical specifications of JavaHelp, you can access technical documents through Sun Microsystems' Java Technology web site at *http://www.javasoft.com.* One technical document in particular you might want to review is the JavaHelp specification.

Assumptions This Book Makes

As you will learn in this book, you must write JavaHelp topics (the actual help topics that make up the JavaHelp system) in HTML. Since this book is about Java-Help and not HTML, it assumes you have a basic understanding of HTML. I'm not saying you have to be a webmaster or an HTML programmer, but you must have a basic understanding of HTML tags and how to use them. I provide ideas on how to format your topics, but I don't stop to explain what the HTML behind them means. If you have no experience with HTML, have no fear. All you will need is a good HTML editor to create your help topics. You may also want to refer to *HTML: The Definitive Guide*, by Chuck Musciano and Bill Kennedy (O'Reilly & Associates), as an HTML reference. I refer to this book many times when creating HTML topic files.

Conventions Used in This Book

The following font conventions are used in this book:

Italic is used for:

- Unix pathnames, filenames, and program names
- Internet addresses, such as domain names and URLs
- New terms where they are defined

Boldface is used for:

- Names of GUI items: window names, buttons, menu choices, etc.

`Constant width` is used for:

- Command lines and options that should be typed verbatim
- Names and keywords in Java programs, including method names, variable names, and class names
- XML element tags

Comments and Questions

The information in this book has been tested and verified, but you may find that features have changed (or you may even find mistakes!). You can send any errors you find, as well as suggestions for future editions, to:

O'Reilly & Associates, Inc.
101 Morris Street
Sebastopol, CA 95472
(800) 998-9938 (in the United States or Canada)
(707) 829-0515 (international/local)
(707) 829-0104 (fax)

You can also send messages electronically. To be put on the mailing list or request a catalog, send email to:

info@oreilly.com

To ask technical questions or comment on the book, send email to:

bookquestions@oreilly.com

There is a web site for the book, where examples, errata, and any plans for future editions are listed. The site also includes a link to a forum where you can discuss the book with the author and other readers. You can access this site at:

http://www.oreilly.com/catalog/creatingjavahelp

For more information about this book and others, see the O'Reilly web site:

http://www.oreilly.com

Acknowledgments

One of the most important chapters in this book, Chapter 7, *Using the JavaHelp API for Advanced Presentation Options*, would not have been possible without Marc Loy. The chapter is technical and required the touch of a talented Java developer. Marc wrote most of the first draft for me to make sure the chapter included the appropriate level of information for Java developers. As part of his work on the chapter, Marc also developed the small sample application that demonstrates the Java code for implementing JavaHelp. Finally, Marc also put together Appendix C, *The Java-Help API*. Thank you, Marc, for being so generous with your time and Java programming talents. This book would not be complete if it weren't for your help.

I am also indebted to Alicia Norton, a colleague and extremely talented technical writer, for reviewing, editing, and testing every chapter of this book while I was writing it. Her efforts helped me turn in cleaner chapters during the writing process. Thank you, Alicia, for your feedback. And thank you for your encouragement throughout the entire book-writing process.

Thanks to O'Reilly—especially Mike Loukides—for your help and for the opportunity to write this book. Thanks to John Posner for all of your editing efforts when I finished the book. Also, thanks to Robert Romano for your help with the illustrations.

Sun Microsystems should be proud of their JavaHelp development team—particularly Larry Hoffman and Roger Brinkley—who answered my many, many emails, often within hours (and sometimes within minutes).

I must express gratitude to Dr. Kristin Woolever, my first technical writing teacher and mentor, for teaching me most of what I know about technical writing. Without you as a role model, Kristin, I would never have learned about computer writing and could never have written this book.

Finally, for all of my friends who had no idea what I've been writing about: read this book, and you'll finally understand what JavaHelp is.

1

Understanding JavaHelp

When I first saw a demonstration of Sun Microsystems' JavaHelp early in 1998, I knew that Sun had designed a great new HTML-based help system that would answer most help authors' needs. They proposed the best online help solution for Java applications and applets, and offered a great source for online help and documentation in general. Finally: online documentation that is easy to author, easy to use, and, best of all, fully functional across all computer platforms.

We are entering an age in software documentation where new HTML-based help systems are emerging and are trying to provide solutions for all help-authoring needs. With Java becoming such a widely used programming language, help authors need an HTML-based help system that is as flexible as the Java applications themselves. JavaHelp to the rescue!

To get you started learning JavaHelp, this chapter provides the following topics:

- What is JavaHelp?
- Using JavaHelp for online documentation
- Understanding the files in a HelpSet
- Following the JavaHelp process
- Installing JavaHelp on your computer
- Seeing JavaHelp in action
- Deciding how to present a HelpSet
- Deciding how to install a HelpSet
- Encapsulating HelpSet files
- Finding more information on JavaHelp

What Is JavaHelp?

JavaHelp is an online help system developed in the Java programming language. It is similar to other help systems, such as WinHelp and HTML Help, in that you use a table of contents (TOC), index, or word-search index to find and display help topics. A complete "online help data set," consisting of individual help-topic files, TOC, and indexes, is called a *HelpSet*.

As shown in Figure 1-1, JavaHelp uses a *tripane* window (a window with three frames), which contains a Toolbar pane, a Navigation pane, and a Content pane. This tripane window, called the *HelpSet Viewer*, offers users the ability to work with the help system's commands, navigation controls, and help topics at the same time, without having to switch to different windows. Using this tripane window, users select an item from the navigation pane, and the corresponding help topic appears in the content pane. If a help topic contains a link, the user can click it to display the corresponding HTML page in the content pane. If the link leads to another topic in the same HelpSet, the navigation pane automatically updates itself to highlight the title of the new topic.

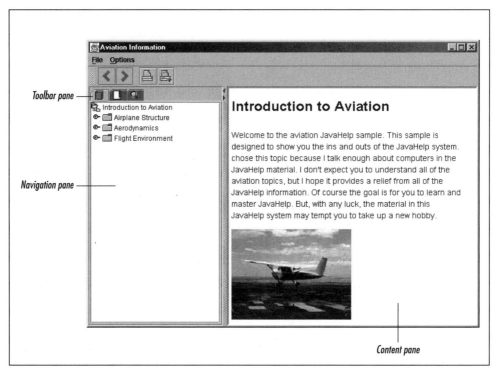

Figure 1-1. The HelpSet Viewer

The HelpSet Viewer functions like a web browser: it has similar controls, but it is designed specifically to work with JavaHelp files.

JavaHelp topic files are HTML files, and these HTML files function the same way as in a web browser. The HelpSet Viewer also supports pop-up windows, secondary windows, and multimedia clips. (Java programming is required to provide a Java multimedia component for use with the HelpSet Viewer.)

Like other help systems, JavaHelp can present help information to users in several ways:

Application-level help
> The user enters at a top level, such as an introductory topic or a table of contents.

Screen-level help
> The user clicks a button to launch the help system with a specific help topic that describes the application's current screen.

Field-level help
> The user selects a specific application control (such as a text box or button) on which to obtain help.

Embedded help
> The help system is built directly into the application's interface.

If you are familiar with other help systems, you might be thinking, "So what's new?" JavaHelp's unique feature is that it is developed in the Java programming language. Therefore, Java programming can enhance the HelpSet Viewer to match your project's custom needs. Also, JavaHelp integrates seamlessly with Java applications. Since JavaHelp runs with the Java platform, it runs in the same process as the Java application for which it is created.

Using JavaHelp for Online Documentation

With so many options for online help systems, you may wonder why you should use JavaHelp or how it compares with other online help systems. JavaHelp may be not only the best online help system to use with your Java applications or applets but also a great source for providing online documentation in general.

Why Use JavaHelp for Online Help?

If you are designing online help for a Java application, JavaHelp is the best help system for the job. Since JavaHelp is written in Java, it is platform-independent and guaranteed to run in any environment in which its associated Java application runs. Also, since JavaHelp is implemented using Java Foundation Class (JFC) components, Java programming can customize JavaHelp's interfaces and functionality.

JavaHelp offers many online help-presentation options. You can design it for standalone, context-sensitive, or embedded modes; you can also use other standard help features such as pop-up windows, secondary windows, and multimedia integration.

Finally, JavaHelp is easy to merge and update. If you have different software applications with different HelpSets, you can merge them so that users see a single, integrated online help system. If you ever have to update your JavaHelp topics, you can easily do so since JavaHelp uses standard HTML files for its help topics.

Comparing JavaHelp with Other Help Systems

Help authors today have many options for providing online documentation. Most help authors are familiar with WinHelp, an older Windows help system that provides online documentation with Windows-based applications. Today there are an increasing number of online help options, most of which are based on HTML. HTML-based help systems (such as JavaHelp) offer online help solutions for more than just the Windows operating system.

Having many online help systems to choose from, however, makes it more confusing for help authors to decide which help system to use under which situation. It is not the position of this book to tell you which help system to use in different situations—only to help you recognize circumstances for which JavaHelp is your best online help solution.

I've already explained why JavaHelp is the perfect solution for Java applications. Actually, JavaHelp will probably solve the majority of your online documentation needs whether you're working with Java applications or not. For example, as you will read in the next section, you can use JavaHelp for online books, such as reference manuals or user's guides.

The only situation where I would *not* recommend using JavaHelp is when you want to incorporate an online help system into a non-Java application. Because of the different environments, other online help systems are better for different platforms. For example, an application developed with Visual Basic would not be well suited for JavaHelp. You could certainly use JavaHelp, but using the Java runtime environment only for the online help system would not be worth the required resources. Instead, a more compatible online help system such as WinHelp or HTML Help would work better with the application and integrate more smoothly with the development environment.

Using JavaHelp for General Online Documentation

JavaHelp is not only a solution for providing online help with Java applications. Since JavaHelp is platform-independent, it offers a solution for general online documentation. Online books and reference material can be distributed through Java-Help, since users of all platforms can access it.

For example, the Aviation document illustrated in Figure 1-1 could be an online reference document independent of any software application. You could create something similar for reference manuals, user's guides, product specifications, and just about any other type of document you can imagine.

When you compare other options for online books, JavaHelp emerges as a viable solution. For example, you could use ASCII text files to distribute cross-platform documentation; however, you would not be able to use user-friendly navigation controls or add images and text formatting as with JavaHelp. If you want to use a more sophisticated documentation tool (such as Microsoft Word) to add navigation, images, and text formatting to your documentation, you have to deal with more complex issues with regards to portability and user software requirements.

Understanding the Files in a HelpSet

Each online help project (such as the Aviation project previously illustrated) is implemented as a set of files, called the *HelpSet*. A HelpSet includes HTML-format topic files along with JavaHelp-specific configuration files.

The HelpSet includes three kinds of files:

- HelpSet data files
- Navigation files
- Topic files

HelpSet data files contain overall information about the structure and content of the HelpSet. These are text files, structured in Extensible Markup Language (XML) format. There are two HelpSet data files:

- The *HelpSet file*, with filename suffix *.hs*, is the HelpSet's "master control" file. It specifies the navigation components to be used, along with the files that configure the navigation components. It also specifies the HelpSet's map file.

    Don't confuse the similar terms *HelpSet file* and *HelpSet*. The *HelpSet* is the set of all files in a particular project; the *HelpSet file* is the project's master control file.

- The *map file*, with filename suffix *.jhm*, assigns a *map ID* (shorthand name) to each help topic. It maps ID strings to the uniform resource locators (URLs) of topic files. The HelpSet file and navigation files always use map IDs to refer to help topics; they never use the topic's URLs directly.

The *navigation files* configure the HelpSet's TOC, index, and word-search index. The TOC and index files (also in XML format) are similar in structure. The Java-Help system reads the information in these files to know what to display in the TOC and index tabs in the navigation pane.

NOTE   What is the difference between "JavaHelp system" and "HelpSet"? I
              use the term JavaHelp system to mean the HelpSet Viewer (or a
              viewer embedded in another application) in action: loading a
              HelpSet, displaying its help topics and enabling the user to navigate
              between topics. The term HelpSet is just the set of files *you* provide
              to implement a particular online help project.

The word-search index is a bit more complex; it refers to a folder that contains several files. You create these files using an indexing utility Sun provides with Java-Help. The indexing utility builds a full-text search database for the HelpSet. The database is then searched when users type in a specific word under the word-search tab in the navigation pane.

The actual topic files for a HelpSet are HTML files. You can have only one topic per HTML file because the map file assigns one map ID to one HTML file. The topic files can include images and links just as with ordinary HTML pages. Additionally, you can use controls for pop-up windows, secondary windows, and multimedia clips.

Following the JavaHelp Process

The JavaHelp system begins by reading a HelpSet file, which provides information about a particular help project. To display navigation information, the JavaHelp system reads the navigation files listed in the HelpSet file. Additionally, the Java-Help system uses the information in the map file to find the individual topic files in the HelpSet. Figure 1-2 demonstrates how the HelpSet files work together to display information in the viewer.

For example, let's say that a person accesses online help to find a help topic on deleting files in an application. When the user opens the HelpSet for that application, the system first reads the HelpSet file and determines the location of the map file and the navigation files. The system then reads those map and navigation files and displays the navigation information in the navigation area of the HelpSet Viewer. The user can then use the navigation components (TOC, index, or word-search index) to find the topic on deleting files. The appropriate help topic then displays in the content area of the HelpSet Viewer.

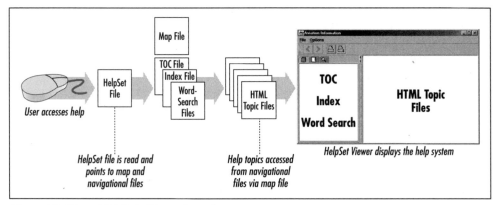

Figure 1-2. How a HelpSet's files work together

Installing JavaHelp on Your Computer

To work with JavaHelp while you read this book, you must set up your computer to run JavaHelp as well as the sample files in this book. You can obtain the JavaHelp distribution from Sun Microsystems' JavaHelp web page at *http://www.java.sun. com/products/javahelp*. Also, I provide a link to Sun's download page under "Examples" on the book's web page, *http://www.oreilly.com/catalog/creatingjavahelp*.

Once you connect to the download site, Sun provides instructions on how to download and run the JavaHelp installation file. Although Sun provides a default installation location, I installed JavaHelp to the root level of my computer. Under Windows, you can install JavaHelp in *C:\jh1.1*; under Unix or Linux, you could install it in subdirectory *jh1.1* of your home directory (or, if you have permission, in */usr/local/jh1.1*). Also, take a peek ahead to Chapter 8, *Deploying the Help System to Your Users*. In the section "Ensuring Basic Java Support," I discuss matching Java-Help to a computer's Java processing environment.

What About JavaHelp 1.0?

JavaHelp 1.0 is no longer available on Sun's JavaHelp web page. Since any work done in JavaHelp 1.0 is completely compatible with JavaHelp 1.1, I highly recommend switching to JavaHelp 1.1 regardless of which Java development environment you use.

When you install the JavaHelp distribution, pay close attention to any *README* file that Sun includes. As JavaHelp is developed further, its requirements may change. For example, the version I used for writing this book required shell commands to

launch a JavaHelp system. However, when Sun released a newer version of Java-
Help, they provided a graphical user interface (GUI) tool to handle this task. The
only way to know what is current is to keep up with Sun's documentation.

After you install JavaHelp, download the sample files used in this book (click on
"Examples" at this book's web page). There are HelpSets and small Java applications, all of which are designed to help you learn JavaHelp. Each set of sample files
is compressed. To use them, decompress the files and read the enclosed *ReadMe.
txt* file for more information.

NOTE   To help you learn JavaHelp concepts, some chapters instruct you to
                change the original code in certain sample files. Before making any
                changes, you should back up the entire folder containing the origi-
                nal files. This backup prevents you from permanently losing the
                files' original information after you modify them. Each exercise
                assumes you are starting with the original files downloaded from this
                book's web site.

Seeing JavaHelp in Action

JavaHelp is intuitive and functions similarly to other online help systems. If you are
familiar with WinHelp or HTML Help, you should have no problem navigating
through a JavaHelp system. This section guides you through working with a Java-
Help system and shows you how JavaHelp's basic features work.

NOTE   If you have not yet downloaded the sample files discussed earlier in
                this chapter, you should do so before continuing. While the screen
                shots in this section provide a sufficient "look" at JavaHelp, only the
                system itself can provide you with its actual "feel."

Starting the JavaHelp System

The way users will start the JavaHelp system depends on how you connect it to an
application or applet. Usually, it is as simple as clicking a button or selecting a
menu item. To run a JavaHelp system independently of an application (for
example, when you are testing a HelpSet), use the *hsviewer* utility Sun includes
with JavaHelp. Under Windows, you can launch the *hsviewer* utility through a
shortcut created in the **Start** menu when you installed JavaHelp. Under Unix or
Linux, you can find *hsviewer* in the *demos/bin* subdirectory in the JavaHelp installation area.

The HelpSet Viewer starts by displaying a simple file-selection dialog. Specify the HelpSet filename and the URL of the directory where it resides, as shown in Figure 1-3.

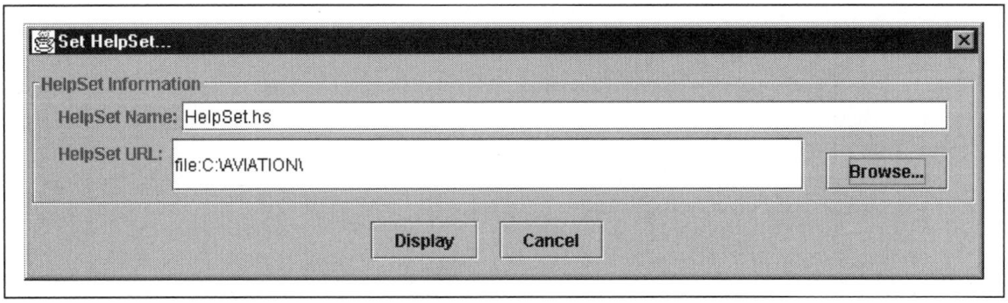

Figure 1-3. HelpSet Viewer: specifying a HelpSet

Give it a try: specify the Aviation HelpSet file and URL in the *hsviewer* utility. The easiest way to do this is to click the **Browse** button and browse for the HelpSet file. Once you have specified the HelpSet name and directory URL, click the **Display** button to load the HelpSet into the JavaHelp system.

Working with the JavaHelp Interface

After you load the Aviation HelpSet, take a look at the HelpSet Viewer's structure. As discussed earlier, the standard HelpSet Viewer uses a tripane window to display its menus, toolbar, navigation controls, and help topics. As you saw in Figure 1-1, the *toolbar pane* contains the menu and toolbar, which offer menus and controls to assist you in viewing the current HelpSet. The *navigation pane* contains a TOC, index, or word-search index. The *content pane* displays the current help topic. You can not only read the topic's content in this pane but can also access pop-up and secondary windows for expanded information, launch multimedia clips (if you have a multimedia component), and follow hyperlinks to other topics or web pages. Hyperlinks can lead not only to HTML pages in the current HelpSet, but also to web sites on the Internet, as shown with the **avbook.com** link in the Aviation introductory topic. (The HelpSet Viewer cannot display all HTML-format files. See Chapter 4, *Preparing Help Topics*, for more information.)

Using Toolbar Controls and Menus

The JavaHelp toolbar contains previous and next buttons, similar to those found in web browsers. The previous and next buttons enable you to browse back and forth through topics you have previously viewed. They do not advance you back and forth in order of the help topics as they exist in the TOC. Like a web browser, these buttons are not enabled until you begin navigating through the help system and have viewed topics to which you can move back and forth.

The toolbar also contains print buttons next to the previous and next buttons. You use the print buttons to set up the page's print options and to print the help topic that is displayed in the HelpSet Viewer.

As you read a help topic, you might find that you would rather display the topic in the entire viewer instead of taking up space for the navigation pane. You can easily show and hide the navigation pane using buttons, as shown in Figure 1-4.

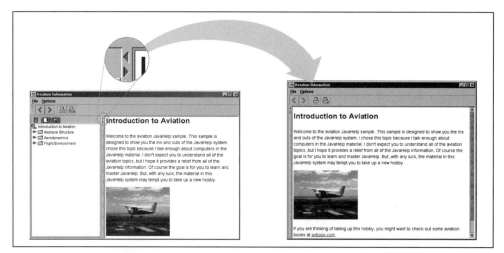

Figure 1-4. HelpSet Viewer: showing and hiding the navigation pane

There are also menus at the top of the HelpSet Viewer. These menus offer basic functions such as opening a web page, selecting a new HelpSet, or setting font preferences. If you click **Open page** from the **File** menu, the HelpSet Viewer displays the window shown in Figure 1-5.

Figure 1-5. HelpSet Viewer: opening a help topic or web page

You can use this window to access not only topics from the current HelpSet but also HTML pages from any web site. If you are connected to the Internet, try typing *http://www.oreilly.com* in the **URL** box and then click the **OK** button. As you probably guessed, the HelpSet Viewer displays the O'Reilly web site.

If you select **Set HelpSet** from the **File** menu, the viewer displays the same window shown in Figure 1-3 for selecting a new HelpSet. You can also change the fonts in the navigation pane by clicking **Set Font** from the **Options** menu. When the **Set Font** window appears, simply select a font and size.

Navigating Through the JavaHelp System

Below the toolbar controls and menus is the navigation pane. The navigation controls are very important in any online documentation system. Online documentation is useless if users cannot find the information they need. As shown earlier in Figure 1-1, the navigation pane in the JavaHelp system provides three types of navigation controls (or *navigators*):

- TOC
- Index
- Word-search index (known as the *Find* feature in other online help systems)

You access each navigation control by clicking its associated tab, as shown in Figure 1-6.

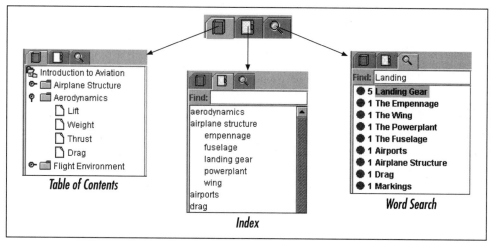

Figure 1-6. JavaHelp navigation controls

The *TOC* provides navigation information similar to the TOC of a book. Individual topics are grouped into categories (like sections of a book are grouped into chapters). Each category (represented in Figure 1-6 by a folder icon) can contain both subcategories and individual topics. You can open and close a category by double-clicking the category name or by single-clicking the level icon to its left. You view a help topic by clicking its title. Give it a try using the following steps with the Aviation HelpSet:

1. Double-click the **Airplane Structure** category in the TOC.

   An overview topic that is associated with the category appears in the content pane, and a list of help topics expands below the **Airplane Structure** folder in the TOC.

2. Click a help topic within the **Airplane Structure** category.

   As you would expect, the associated topic appears in the content pane.

3. Now is a good time to use the previous and next buttons in the toolbar to see how they integrate with the TOC. Click the previous button.

   The content pane "jumps" (backward or forward) to the previously displayed topic. Notice that the highlighted category or topic in the TOC stays synchronized with the topic displayed in the content pane.

The *index* provides navigation information similar to the index of a book, with one distinct difference: in the JavaHelp index, you can type a word, or any character string, directly to find it in the index. Under the index tab (the middle tab), in the **Find** box, type the word `landing` (the index is case-sensitive, so be sure to use all lowercase letters as shown) and press Enter. The system highlights the first index item that matches the search string, and the index item's associated topic displays in the content pane.

With `landing` still typed in the **Find** box, press Enter again. As you keep pressing Enter, subsequent index items are highlighted in the index and their associated topics display in the content pane. You can also scroll through the index to select items from it.

JavaHelp also offers a *word-search index* facility through which users can type a word or phrase and have the system display a choice of topics that contain that word or phrase. The search is case-insensitive. The helpfulness of this feature depends on the search term the user types. With a specific term, such as "metadata file," the word-search facility will probably find just the desired topics. With a general term, such as "file," the word-search facility will probably find too many topics.

Give this feature a try with the Aviation HelpSet. Under the word-search index tab (the tab on the right), in the **Find** box, type `retractable landing gear` and then press Enter. The result of the word search is a list of topics. Each topic is annotated with the number of *hits*—the number of occurrences of the search term, exactly or approximately, within the topic.

The HelpSet Viewer automatically displays the first help topic in the list of hits, with the occurrences of the search term highlighted. In the navigation pane, each hit is annotated with a number and an icon. The number indicates how often the search term appears in the help topic; the icon represents the *ranking* of that topic's matches, i.e., how close the text in the topic is to the specified search term. There are five possible rankings, from a full circle (highest ranking) to an empty circle (lowest ranking).

For example, when you enter the phrase `retractable landing gear`, the viewer generates several topic titles. The title "Landing Gear" has a full circle because all of the words in the search phrase ("retractable," "landing," and "gear") appear in the topic together. The title "Drag" has a half-filled circle because only two of the words ("landing" and "gear") appear in the topic. The title "Airports" has an almost empty circle because only one word ("landing") appears in the topic.

Viewing Help Topics

When you access help topics using navigation controls, you can work with them as if they were in a standard web browser. You can scroll through and read topics the same way you do with a web browser. Also, hyperlinks work the same way as in a browser. When you see blue underlined text in a topic, click it to go to the topic associated with that link. You can access pop-up windows, secondary windows, and multimedia clips through help topics. To see how these features work, go through the following steps with the Aviation HelpSet:

1. If it is not already selected, click **Introduction to Aviation**.

2. When the help topic opens, click the **JavaHelp Note** button.

   A pop-up window appears, providing a note. You are not limited to buttons for providing pop-up windows; you can also use an image or a regular text link.

3. Click anywhere in the HelpSet Viewer (but not in the pop-up window) to close the pop-up window.

4. Click the TOC folder titled **Airplane Structure**.

5. When the help topic opens, click the picture of the airplane.

   A similar pop-up window appears.

6. Click anywhere in the HelpSet Viewer to close the pop-up window.

7. In the TOC, open the folders **Flight Environment**, **Airports**, and then **Runways and Taxiways**, and then click the TOC help topic titled **Markings**.

8. When the help topic opens, click the bulleted blue text "Runway markings."

This time a secondary window appears. Notice that this window looks more like a standard window than did the pop-up window. You can move, resize, and close the secondary window like a standard window.

9. Close the secondary window by clicking its close button.

I discuss pop-up windows and secondary windows in more detail in Chapter 6, *Enhancing the HelpSet*.

Deciding How to Present a HelpSet

The way you present a HelpSet to users can be as important as the help content itself. If users have a hard time accessing the help system, they might become reluctant to use it. The main presentation options for a HelpSet are standalone help, context-sensitive help (screen-level or field-level), and embedded help.

Using Standalone Help

A standalone HelpSet is one that the user views independently of an application. When the user calls for help (either while running the application or at another time), the HelpSet Viewer appears with an overview topic in the content pane. From this initial point, users must navigate through the help system to find the topics in which they are interested. Navigation controls are very important to a standalone HelpSet, because they are the only means the user has to access detailed information.

The Aviation HelpSet used in this book is an example of a standalone HelpSet. You launch it manually and then navigate through the HelpSet's topics. A straight-forward alternative is to have an application launch a standalone HelpSet when the user invokes the application's help command.

Using Context-Sensitive Help

Standalone HelpSets are sufficient for supporting an application, but what if you want to provide a friendlier help system to your users? You might want to provide help through context-sensitivity. Context-sensitivity simply means that the help system displays a help topic specific to the given situation at the time the user requests help. There are two types of context-sensitive help, both are available with JavaHelp. The first type is called *screen-level* help. With screen-level context-sensitive help, the user is working in a particular application screen that has a button to activate help. When the user clicks that button, the help system starts and displays the specific help topic for the active screen. The user can also navigate through the help system to view other topics.

The second type of context-sensitive help is called *field-level* help (also known as What's This help). This type of help is integrated with the application's interface. Users typically activate a mechanism (for example, clicking a button with a question mark) and then point to or click a control in the active window. The help system then displays a help topic that describes the selected control.

Some help systems use a simple pop-up window for field-level help to save screen space. With JavaHelp, invoking field-level help launches the full HelpSet Viewer and displays the topic for that particular control. Although this method takes up more screen space and operating-system resources, it offers users an easy way to access related topics.

Using Embedded Help

Another way to increase user-friendliness is with embedded help. Embedded help is similar to context-sensitive help in that it displays the help topic associated with the current condition of the application. The difference is that embedded help is built into the interface so that the user sees it all the time. As the user switches to different windows or controls, the help remains visible, but the active topic changes to reflect the changes in the application's condition.

In general, embedded help does not necessarily look like a traditional help system. Help can come in the form of icons, tips, numbered arrows, or any visual device built into the application's interface. With JavaHelp, however, embedded help is more limited: it is visual JavaHelp components (content pane, navigation pane) built directly into a Java application's user interface.

Deciding How to Install a HelpSet

JavaHelp itself is network-capable: the HelpSet Viewer can load a HelpSet from the computer where it is running or from a remote computer. When deciding how to install a particular HelpSet, take into account the network-capability of the application for which you're providing help. The following sections present appropriate installation decisions for several kinds of applications.

Local Application

A local application is one that runs on the user's computer *without* interaction with any other computer (via a web browser or other type of network connection). When users request help, the application launches the help system locally—that is, on the same computer. In this situation, it is best to install the application and your HelpSet together on the computer, in a single installation process. If the application doesn't rely on access to a network, neither should the help system.

Network Application

In a network application, users might have a small part of the application installed on their computer (the client) and access the rest of the application on one main computer on the network (the server). Since a network is required to run the application, it makes sense to install the HelpSet on the server. When users access help on the client computer, the request goes across the network to access the necessary HelpSet files on the server, and then returns the information to display it in the HelpSet Viewer on the client.

I recommend this installation option for any network application. Since users must be connected to the server to run the application, it makes sense to take advantage of the larger disk space usually associated with network servers. What about the performance hit? In most corporate networks, the delay involved in accessing the help files across the network should be quite acceptable. Any performance issues are probably outweighed by the advantages in disk usage and administration. It would be a waste to install the HelpSet on multiple client computers when you have the option to install them once, on the server. If you need to update the HelpSet files later, you can do so in one location instead of multiple locations.

Java Applet

A Java applet is an application that runs within a web browser. This probably means that the user's computer is on a corporate network (intranet) or on the Internet. In this case, you should install the HelpSet that documents the applet on the server, as described in the earlier section "Network Application", and have the applet access the HelpSet across the network. In the less typical case where the applet is located on the local computer, you should install the applet's HelpSet locally, as described in the previous section "Local Application."

Java Product Suite

Some applications have multiple Java components, each with its own online help—for example, an office suite application. The separate components of the suite might include a word processor, a spreadsheet application, and a database application. Each component would have its own HelpSet.

Since the components are part of a larger application, you might want to merge all the HelpSets together, presenting a single, integrated help system to the user.

Encapsulating HelpSet Files

A HelpSet consists of multiple files—one for each help topic, one for each graphic, and several JavaHelp-specific files (HelpSet file, map file, etc.). In designing your installation strategy, consider whether you want to *encapsulate* all these files into a single Java archive (JAR) file. To minimize storage requirements, the utility that creates a JAR file compresses the data automatically.

Even if you have never heard of JAR files before, you might be more familiar with them than you think. JAR files are very similar to the popular ZIP files. In fact, if you have a ZIP utility, you can decompress and examine the contents of JAR files.

JavaHelp works the same way, whether or not you install the HelpSet as a JAR file. The only difference is that the HelpSet Viewer must extract individual HelpSet files from the JAR file, which involves a minor performance hit. In Chapter 8, I discuss JAR compression in greater detail and provide tips for when and when not to use JAR files.

Finding More Information on JavaHelp

When you have completed this book (or better yet, while you are reading it) you can obtain the latest JavaHelp information from Sun Microsystems' web site, which contains the following sources of JavaHelp-related information:

- The official JavaHelp site, located at *http://www.java.sun.com/products/ javahelp*. The JavaHelp site offers current news such as upcoming JavaHelp releases, JavaHelp events, and involvement with third-party vendors. You can also join the JavaHelp mailing list from this site.

- The Java Developer Connection (JDC), which is free to join and is located at *http://developer.javasoft.com*. The JDC offers access to technical information such as the JavaHelp specification.

- The JavaHelp discussion group, which is part of the JDC. To access this discussion group, click the **Toolbar** option at the JDC site to launch the JDC Applet Toolbar. From this toolbar you can run the Java GroupReader applet, which displays a list of discussion groups, including the JavaHelp discussion group. For information on using the GroupReader applet, connect to the Group-Reader applet site at *http://developer.java.sun.com/developer/GroupReader.html*.

2

Creating Your
First HelpSet

Now that you have a basic understanding of how JavaHelp works, it's time to build a small HelpSet. The purpose of this chapter is to give you some practical experience with JavaHelp before you study it in more detail. This chapter is "hands on": it walks you through the development process without lengthy explanations of the concepts behind it. The rest of this book then expands on the procedures you learn here, providing the detailed information you need to thoroughly understand JavaHelp development.

The HelpSet you'll build in this chapter—we'll call it MyJavaHelp—is even simpler than the Aviation sample introduced in Chapter 1, *Understanding JavaHelp*. But the procedures for building it are nearly the same as those for building a more complex HelpSet.

To best understand the structure of HelpSet data and navigation files, you should create them on your own. However, since the topic files are in basic HTML format, you might want to simply download the file set from this book's web page instead of creating them all from scratch: click on "Examples" at *http://www.oreilly.com/catalog/creatingjavahelp*.

At the end of this chapter, you will have a functioning JavaHelp system. To get you there, this chapter provides procedures to guide you through the following Java-Help development processes:

- Creating the HelpSet's directory structure
- Creating HelpSet data and navigation files
- Creating help topic files
- Checking your work
- Testing the finished HelpSet

Creating the HelpSet's Directory Structure

To access HelpSet files, JavaHelp depends on proper file and directory structure. Referring to a file by the wrong name or placing a file in a wrong directory, causes JavaHelp to fail when it tries to access the file. To ensure accurate file retrieval, start your project by setting up the HelpSet's entire directory structure. Figure 2-1 shows the directory and file structure you'll create for MyJavaHelp.

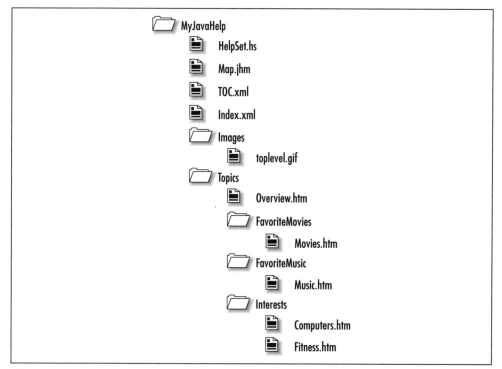

Figure 2-1. Structure of the MyJavaHelp HelpSet

In general, you can use whatever directory and filenames you like. However, keep in mind the following:

- It's best to use the filename extensions shown in Figure 2-1.

- If you rename any data or navigation files (i.e., *Map.jhm, TOC.xml, Index.xml*), you must edit the HelpSet file, *HelpSet.hs*, which contains references to these files.

Figure 2-1 shows a directory, *Topics*, which contains three subdirectories (*FavoriteMovies, FavoriteMusic*, and *Interests*). In general, you can use any number of directories and subdirectories, nested to any depth. Chapter 3, *Planning the Java-Help Project*, provides strategies for planning the organization of your file directories and options for arranging your files. In this chapter, you'll use a very simple structure.

Start the project by creating the directory structure shown in Figure 2-1. First, create *MyJavaHelp*, the master directory that will hold all the data for the HelpSet. Within the *MyJavaHelp* directory, create the following subdirectories:

- *Images* (to hold image files)
- *Topics* (to hold help topic files)

Place the *toplevel.gif* image inside the *Images* directory by copying it from the Java-Help installation area (filename *jh1.1\Demos\hs\holidays\images\toplevel.gif*). This image file is the icon that appears at the top level of the TOC in the HelpSet Viewer.

In the *Topics* directory, create the subdirectories that will contain the actual help topic files: *FavoriteMovies, FavoriteMusic,* and *Interests*

NOTE   Try to be consistent in devising directory names and filenames. This will help you avoid spelling errors. The name of each subdirectory contains one or more capitalized words, with no intervening spaces. This style makes a directory name easy to read and clearly indicates the directory's contents

---

You now have the entire directory structure required for the MyJavaHelp HelpSet.

Creating HelpSet Data and Navigation Files

A HelpSet contains a set of topic files, along with a number of data and navigation files. The topic files are in HTML format; the data and navigation files are in XML (Extensible Markup Language) format. XML looks similar to HTML, but has application-specific tags, such as `<mapID>` and `<tocitem>`, instead of HTML's standardized document-formatting tags, such as `<head>` and `<p>`.

Each data and navigation file contains XML *elements*, most of which take the following form:

```
<element-name  attr-name="attr-value"  attr-name="attr-value"/>
```

Here, "attr" means "attribute." Each element can have any number of attributes, including none at all. The value of each attribute must be enclosed in single or double quotes. XML elements are like HTML *tags* (at least as far as JavaHelp is concerned).

Creating the HelpSet File

Using your text editor, create the file *HelpSet.hs* in the *MyJavaHelp* directory, with the following contents. Be sure the capitalization is correct: XML is case-sensitive!

```
<?xml version='1.0' encoding='ISO-8859-1' ?>
<!DOCTYPE helpset
    PUBLIC "-//Sun Microsystems Inc.//DTD JavaHelp HelpSet Version 1.0//EN"
           "http://java.sun.com/products/javahelp/helpset_1_0.dtd">

<helpset version="1.0">
  <title>My JavaHelp System</title>
  <maps>
    <mapref location="Map.jhm"/>
    <homeID>overview</homeID>
  </maps>
  <view>
    <name>TOC</name>
    <label>TOC</label>
    <type>javax.help.TOCView</type>
    <data>TOC.xml</data>
  </view>
  <view>
    <name>Index</name>
    <label>Index</label>
    <type>javax.help.IndexView</type>
    <data>Index.xml</data>
  </view>
</helpset>
```

This file specifies the names of the other data and navigation files for the MyJava-Help HelpSet: *Map.jhm, TOC.xml*, and *Index.xml*. You'll create these files in the sections that follow.

NOTE   In this file, as in all XML-format configuration files, it doesn't matter whether you indent elements with spaces or tabs. But doing so *does* help humans read the file, since it shows how some elements are logically contained within others.

Creating the Map File

The map file assigns a unique keyword (called a *map ID*) to each topic file in the HelpSet, using `mapID` elements:

```
<mapID target="fitness" url="Topics/Interests/Fitness.htm"/>
```

Creating a map file can be long and tedious for a HelpSet with many topic files, but it is easy for MyJavaHelp, which is very small. For simplicity, use each topic file-name (without the extension) as its map ID.

Using a text editor, create the file *Map.jhm* in the *MyJavaHelp* directory, with the following contents:

```
<?xml version='1.0' encoding='ISO-8859-1' ?>
<!DOCTYPE map
  PUBLIC "-//Sun Microsystems Inc.//DTD JavaHelp Map Version 1.0//EN"
         "http://java.sun.com/products/javahelp/map_1_0.dtd">

<map version="1.0">
  <mapID target="toplevelfolder" url="Images/toplevel.gif" />
  <mapID target="overview" url="Topics/Overview.htm"/>
  <mapID target="computers" url="Topics/Interests/Computers.htm"/>
  <mapID target="fitness" url="Topics/Interests/Fitness.htm"/>
  <mapID target="movies" url="Topics/FavoriteMovies/Movies.htm"/>
  <mapID target="music" url="Topics/FavoriteMusic/Music.htm"/>
</map>
```

The URLs in this map file are *relative* pathnames—they are relative to the directory in which the map file resides. Thus, these URLs rely on the *Topics* subdirectory being in the same directory as the *Map.jhm* file (the *MyJavaHelp* directory). However, if an image or topic file were in another directory or at some other site on the Web, you would have to use an *absolute* path, as shown in the following example:

```
<mapID target="overview" url=" http://www.kevinlewis.com/download/overview.htm"/>
```

NOTE   In a map file, you must use forward slashes (/) instead of back-slashes (\) in the values of url attributes. That is, you specify a URL just as you would in a web browser. Also, be aware of case-sensitivity. Windows systems are case-insensitive in reading filenames (and thus, URLs); Unix systems, however, are case-sensitive. It's best to be conservative: always specify file and directory names paying close attention to case.

Creating the Navigation Files

Navigation is an important part of any online help system. The MyJavaHelp HelpSet you are creating in this chapter is quite small, so users could easily find each topic even if you provided only a table of contents (TOC). But imagine trying to find a topic in a HelpSet that contains 200, 500, or more topics. With larger HelpSets, the user is dependent on a complete and usable navigation system.

Even though your HelpSet is small, you should still create a complete navigation facility, including at least a TOC and index. You could also create a word-search index, but I'll defer that discussion until Chapter 5, *Creating HelpSet Data and Navigation Files*.

Creating the TOC file

The TOC file uses a different set of XML elements from the map file. Using your text editor, create the file *TOC.xml* in the *MyJavaHelp* directory, with the following contents:

```
<?xml version='1.0' encoding='ISO-8859-1' ?>
<!DOCTYPE toc
   PUBLIC "-//Sun Microsystems Inc.//DTD JavaHelp TOC Version 1.0//EN"
          "http://java.sun.com/products/javahelp/toc_1_0.dtd">

<toc version="1.0">
<tocitem image="toplevelfolder" target="overview" text="My JavaHelp System">
    <tocitem text="Interests">
      <tocitem target="fitness" text="Fitness"/>
      <tocitem target="computers" text="Computers"/>
    </tocitem>
    <tocitem text="Favorite Movies">
      <tocitem target="movies" text="Favorite Movies"/>
    </tocitem>
    <tocitem text="Favorite Music">
      <tocitem target="music" text="Favorite Music"/>
    </tocitem>
</tocitem>
</toc>
```

(This is an example of a place where indentation style is critical to human readability. "When nesting gets deep, the tough reach for the Tab key.") You probably recognize the map IDs you created in the preceding section. I'll go into more detail about the TOC and other navigation files in Chapter 5. For now, note that:

- The `text` attribute of a `tocitem` element specifies the title to appear in the TOC as displayed by the HelpSet Viewer.

- Some `tocitem` elements are nested within other `tocitem` elements. Nesting of elements represents the hierarchy of the TOC.

Creating the Index File

The index file resembles the TOC in structure and format. But keep in mind that JavaHelp doesn't automatically alphabetize the index items. The order of items in the index file is the order in which the items appear in the HelpSet Viewer. You'll want to allocate time (and/or help-authoring tools, as described in Chapter 9,

Using Third-Party Help-Authoring Tools) for ensuring that the index items are in alphabetical order in the index file.

Using your text editor, create the file *Index.xml* in the *MyJavaHelp* directory, with the following contents:

```
<?xml version='1.0' encoding='ISO-8859-1' ?>
<!DOCTYPE index
  PUBLIC "-//Sun Microsystems Inc.//DTD JavaHelp Index Version 1.0//EN"
        "http://java.sun.com/products/javahelp/index_1_0.dtd">

<index version="1.0">
  <indexitem target="computers" text="computer interests"/>
  <indexitem text="favorites">
    <indexitem target="movies" text="movies"/>
    <indexitem target="music" text="music"/>
  </indexitem>
  <indexitem target="fitness" text="fitness interests"/>
  <indexitem text="interests">
    <indexitem target="computers" text="computers"/>
    <indexitem target="fitness" text="fitness"/>
  </indexitem>
  <indexitem target="movies" text="movies, favorite"/>
  <indexitem target="music" text="music, favorite"/>
  <indexitem target="overview" text="overview"/>
</index>
```

As in the TOC file, the `text` attribute specifies the item to be displayed in the HelpSet Viewer. Nesting of `indexitem` elements defines primary and secondary index items. In this file, `interests` is a primary index item, and `computers` and `fitness` are secondary items.

Creating Help Topic Files

In JavaHelp, the contents of each help topic is defined by a file in HTML format. In this sense, JavaHelp's HelpSet Viewer is very much like a web browser.

In this section, you'll create the individual help topic files. As I mentioned before, if you want to save yourself the time and effort of typing a lot of HTML-format text, simply use the HTML topic files available under "Examples" on this book's web page.

You've already declared, in the map file, both the names and the directory locations of the following MyJavaHelp topic files:

- File *Overview.htm* in the *Topics* directory (see Example 2-1)

- File *Fitness.htm* in the *Interests* subdirectory of the *Topics* directory (see Example 2-2)

- File *Computers.htm* in the *Interests* subdirectory of the *Topics* directory (see Example 2-3)

- File *Movies.htm* in the *FavoriteMovies* subdirectory of the *Topics* directory (see Example 2-4)

- File *Music.htm* in the *FavoriteMovies* subdirectory of the *Topics* directory (see Example 2-5)

Example 2-1. Overview.htm

```
<html>
<head>
<title>Overview</title>
</head>
<body>
<h1>Overview</h1>
<p>Welcome to my JavaHelp system. In this help system I discuss
my interests in the following topics:
<ul>
  <li>Fitness</li>
  <li>Computers</li>
  <li>Movies</li>
  <li>Music</li>
</ul>
</body>
</html>
```

Example 2-2. Fitness.htm

```
<html>
<head>
<title>Fitness</title>
</head>
<body>
<h1>Fitness</h1>
<p>I enjoy the following fitness activities:
<ul>
  <li>Running</li>
  <li>Biking</li>
  <li>Hiking</li>
  <li>Swimming</li>
</ul>
</body>
</html>
```

Example 2-3. Computers.htm

```
<html>
<head>
<title>Computers</title>
```

Example 2-3. Computers.htm (continued)

```
</head>
<body>
<h1>Computers</h1>
<p>I use computers every day for both work and pleasure.</p>
</body>
</html>
```

Example 2-4. Movies.htm

```
<html>
<head>
<title>Favorite Movies</title>
</head>
<body>
<h1>Favorite Movies</h1>
<p>The following movies are some of my favorites:
<ul>
  <li>Titanic</li>
  <li>Sphere</li>
  <li>Halloween</li>
  <li>48 Hours</li>
</ul>
</body>
</html>
```

Example 2-5. Music.htm

```
<html>
<head>
<title>Favorite Music</title>
</head>
<body>
<h1>Favorite Music</h1>
<p>I enjoy the following types of music:
<ul>
  <li>Rock and roll</li>
  <li>Pop</li>
  <li>Easy listening</li>
  <li>Jazz</li>
</ul>
<p>You should also see my list of <a href="../FavoriteMovies/Movies.htm">
favorite movies</a>.</p>
</body>
</html>
```

Checking Your Work

That's all there is to creating the MyJavaHelp HelpSet. Because the directory and file structure is crucial for successfully running the help system, you should double-check your HelpSet's structure. Make sure it matches the structure shown in Figure 2-1.

Testing the Finished HelpSet

You can view your HelpSet the same way you viewed the Aviation HelpSet in the preceding chapter. Start the *hsviewer* utility that comes with JavaHelp and specify *HelpSet.hs* in the *MyJavaHelp* directory as the HelpSet file.

Try out the different navigation components. If the HelpSet Viewer is not already displaying the TOC, click the **TOC** tab to view it. Notice the top-level directory image on the first line in the TOC. This image is the *toplevel.gif* file you copied to your *Images* directory. Open a folder in the TOC, and click one of the topics to display it in the content pane.

Now click the **Index** tab. In the **Find** box, type the word `interests` and then press the Enter or Return key. Notice that JavaHelp highlights the entry in the index. Click any index entry to display its corresponding topic in the content pane.

Congratulations! You (and JavaHelp) have just created a functional help system.

3

Planning the JavaHelp Project

The secret of any successful project, whether it's writing online help or building a house, is good planning. Imagine you want to drive across the country, and you decide to just jump in the car and start driving. Unless you've made the same trip several times in the recent past, you probably won't reach your destination without encountering major problems.

Developing online help is no different. Unless you have a solid plan for your project, you will likely encounter many problems. These problems can add up and negatively affect your final online help system. Project planning helps ensure that your JavaHelp project runs smoothly and that you end up with a usable online help system. It won't remove all obstacles, but good project planning will help you avoid unforeseen problems.

This chapter is about JavaHelp project planning. If you are an experienced help author, you may already have a project-planning system that works well for you. If so, you may want to skim through the chapter and look for sections that are specific to JavaHelp development. If you are new to help-authoring, you should read the entire chapter. It provides a general explanation of project planning by discussing the following topics:

- General planning tasks
- Planning tasks specific to JavaHelp

> *TIP*　　　When planning your project, consider using a third-party help-authoring tool to make help-authoring easier. Third-party tools automate many of the tasks for JavaHelp that would otherwise be tedious and time-consuming. Chapter 9, *Using Third-Party Help-Authoring Tools*, covers JavaHelp-authoring tools and explains why you should understand how JavaHelp works even when using a help-authoring tool to create a HelpSet.

General Planning Tasks

Project planning is highly subjective. If you ask several help authors how to plan a project, you'll probably get several different answers. These differences can be both good and bad. Differences in opinion and new ideas are what drive theory and technology forward. However, for a new help author trying to get some direction on how to plan a new online help project, mixed opinions could only complicate matters. In the following sections, I compare several project-planning theories. My intent is not to claim that other theories are wrong but instead to help you determine a good practice for yourself.

Project planning is quite involved—so involved that authors write entire books on the subject. Since this book is about developing JavaHelp projects, I discuss only project-planning topics I think will help you develop a solid JavaHelp project. If you find a need or desire to learn more about project planning, I encourage you to pick up a book on the subject. In this section, I discuss some general concepts of project planning for online help systems.

Defining the Audience

Before you can outline or write online help topics, you must know the audience of the help system. Start your project by defining your audience. Doing so will help you determine the content of your online help topics, the audience's experience level, any additional elements you should include (such as images or multimedia), the way the audience should access the help system, and any special considerations for navigation. Careful audience definition will help you accurately perform the rest of the project planning and online help development tasks.

> *NOTE*　　　In most cases, defining the audience of an online help system essentially means defining the users of the software for which the help is written. For this reason, I use the words *audience* and *users* interchangeably.

There are many ways to learn about your audience. The important thing is to use all possible resources to find as much information about them as possible. Depending on the resources you have available, you should consider the following options for learning about your audience:

Study user information based on previous releases of similar software
>   If you are writing or updating online help for a software upgrade, use audience information from the previous release such as interviews, surveys, customer-support calls, or any other source of user feedback. If your application is new, you can look at online help from competitors' software, which may help you understand the types of users who may work with your application.

Talk with customer or technical support personnel, who interact with users on a regular basis
>   Customer or technical support personnel frequently talk with users who generally call in with problems or other feedback. Use their information and incorporate it into your online help systems. In the long run, you'll increase user satisfaction and help cut down on support calls.

Talk with marketing personnel, who may have already conducted studies on their users
>   Marketing personnel should know everything about the people buying their software. Talk with them to get information based on research they may have performed to market the product.

Talk with software developers who have conducted their own user studies
>   Software developers are in the same situation as you. They must study the potential users of their software to know how they should develop the application. Sharing information with them provides shortcuts and saves time for the entire development team.

Talk with trainers who have taught classes for the users of your software
>   Because of the nature of classroom interaction, trainers probably know the questions most frequently asked by your users. Talk with them and generate a list of frequently asked questions. Use this information when planning the topics for your HelpSet.

Assess the nature of the software
>   Look at the software itself to define the audience. For example, if the software is a sophisticated data-warehousing tool, you know your audience consists of database programmers and other technical people. On the other hand, if the software is an S.A.T. preparation course, your audience consists of high-school students who are preparing for college. The language you use for these two audience types and the experience level you assume are completely different.

Determining the Audience's Needs

Once you have determined your audience, you can define their needs. There are many aspects to consider when defining the audience's needs. You must consider every situation your users are in as they use the software and access its online help. Consider the following factors as you define your audience's needs:

Input from users

Some companies perform complete needs analyses by talking with potential users of their application. If you are part of such a company, you can ask those users what they need and want in an online help system.

Need for context-sensitive and embedded help

Depending on the users of your software, context-sensitive and embedded help can be a great service. People with little computer experience would welcome such help because it reduces their workload. With context-sensitive help, the system displays the appropriate information based on the application's current situation. Embedded help makes using online help easy since it's always displayed. Context-sensitive and embedded help are usually welcomed by novice users, who need a lot of assistance. However, expert users might become a bit annoyed with embedded help if the application is always forcing online help on them.

Experience level of users

I just mentioned one example of considering different users' experience levels. There are, however, many more considerations. The style you use to write every help topic depends on the experience level of your users. Experienced users are comfortable with technical terms, while novice users need concepts presented in simple terms. Be sure to gear your information toward the right user level. Always plan for the "lowest common denominator." If you have a mix of users, make sure you write for the lowest experience level and use an intuitive navigation design so that users of all experience levels can find the appropriate information.

Age of users

You should consider the age of your users when writing your help topics. The language and tone you use in your writing will be different for a teenager than for an elderly person. The way you come across to your audience determines the credibility you establish with them.

Situation under which users work with the application

The situations under which users work with your application will dictate a large amount of their needs. For example, if the application supports work performed in an office or other business setting, users are probably rushed while working with the application. If users work with the application at home, they are probably not as rushed. You could probably imagine the difference in the way you would have to deliver online help for an application that helps air traffic controllers land aircraft compared to an application that helps people plan a family vacation.

Any disabilities or challenges the user may have

Don't overlook the possibility of disabilities your users might have. Simple tasks, such as moving the mouse and clicking a button, can be difficult for people with certain physical disabilities. If your software is designed to assist people with physical disabilities, you should consider how embedded and context-sensitive help could work with the application. Embedded and context-sensitive help can relieve the user of having to frequently access help and search for specific topics.

Planning Integration with Hardcopy Documentation

A misconception among some help authors is that you can simply convert hardcopy documentation to electronic documentation, throw in a TOC and index, and then end up with a usable online help system. This practice does little to help your audience. The way people use online help is very different from the way they use hardcopy documentation. You therefore must consider how your online help will integrate with any hardcopy documentation included with your application.

A common-sense approach is to think about how you read documentation yourself. When you first purchase software and want to read overview material to understand the basic concepts of how the application works, you probably don't want to run the online help and start reading a lengthy explanation on the screen. Instead, you probably would rather open up a book, grab a comfortable seat, and read about the basics of the application. Conversely, if you are in the middle of a procedure with the application and quickly need to refer to instructions, you don't want to interrupt your workflow to go grab a book off the shelf. Instead, you want to click a button that launches the online help and view the instructions while working with the application.

When planning the content of your online help system, you should determine if certain material should be presented online or if it would be better presented in a book. In general, the following types of information work well in online help:

- Short, general concepts that help users better understand the tasks they are trying to perform

- Procedures for tasks

- Brief reference material

- Troubleshooting information for performing tasks

Notice that for troubleshooting information I said *for performing tasks*. Troubleshooting for system problems (as opposed to task-related problems) should be placed in a hardcopy manual. If users have problems and can't run the software application, they might not be able to access the application's online help. System-related troubleshooting information does little good in a help system if users can't access it.

You should also consider whether or not you will be providing context-sensitive help. There is no need to explain the application's windows and controls in hardcopy documentation if you will be doing so with field-level help. Users want to know what controls do when they are thinking of using them—not when they are trying to understand the basics of the application.

One trick I use when deciding how to integrate the online help with hardcopy documentation is to picture the user reading the online help while working with the application and trying to accomplish a task. I then picture the same user reading nonreference hardcopy documents (such as a user's guide or getting-started book) away from the computer. From these models, I decide what information users need in each situation and place the information appropriately.

Creating an Outline

Before you put your online help system together, create an outline. The outline will be the blueprint for your online help system. A good outline should include every aspect of your help system including types of help topics, content, navigational structure, images, multimedia, and other enhancements you need for your system.

During the project-planning stage, you probably won't know everything about the application for which you are writing help. For this reason, you can't expect your outline to include a list of every help topic in the final HelpSet. Instead, come up with general subjects from which you can develop the final help topics. You should also consider the need for images, multimedia, and other enhancements. You will need to have an idea of the quantity of these enhancements so that you can estimate their development time when you create a schedule.

One important aspect to consider is how the users will access the help system. If the help system supports a web-based applet, and users will be connecting to the Web with a modem, you have to plan a system with smaller files. Using a modem, your audience won't want to wait for larger files to download. This demand requires you to minimize the use of larger files such as images and multimedia. If your users access the applet through a local network, you can afford to use larger files since there is usually little download time over local networks.

Another consideration is whether the users install the application directly on their computer. In this situation, you need to consider the size of your files, not because of their download time, but because you don't want a lot of space taken up by help files. If you plan on using multimedia, consider storing the multimedia files on a CD-ROM and accessing them from the CD-ROM as needed.

Of course, these scenarios reflect only a fraction of the possible needs your users may have. The bottom line is that your outline must account for the needs you determine in the early planning stages. The best way to demonstrate the outline is through an example.

Example of a general outline

Suppose you want to create an outline for the online help system of a word processing application. You would first outline the types of help topics, along with their general content. You would probably decide to have field-level help for every control on every screen in the application. This type of help would contain only brief descriptions of the controls' functions. You would also want to estimate how many controls are needed for field-level help. This knowledge will help you later when you schedule your project tasks.

You also should have conceptual and procedural help—the type of help users see when they click a **Help** button. You would probably decide that you want conceptual and procedural help for topics such as creating new documents, formatting text, using editing tools, incorporating images, as well as other topics related to the word-processing application. Again, you should try to estimate the number of help topics you will need to schedule the project tasks.

The application will run directly on the user's computer, so you don't have to worry about download time for images. You might decide to use multimedia clips since you found that many novice users new to word processing will be using the application. To provide multimedia, you will want to plan on incorporating the clips on a CD-ROM. You will probably end up with an outline similar to the one shown in Figure 3-1. In reality, of course, your outline would be much longer since you would have more topics and longer descriptions.

Testing Your Outline

Once you have an outline, you should test it. There are many ways to test your outline depending on available time and resources. If you have minimal time and resources, a test can be as simple as giving the outline to potential users to see if the proposed system answers their questions. If you have ample time and resources, the test could mean setting up a role-playing environment where users

Help Topic Types:
- Field-level
- Conceptual
- Procedural

Field-Level Help Screens

Desktop
> Controls include the following buttons: New, Open, Save, Print, Print Preview.

Graphics layout
> Controls include the following buttons: Paintbrush, Import, Crop.

Conceptual Help Topics

Creating new documents
> Topics will include how to create new documents from scratch and how to use templates for new documents. Use graphics to demonstrate templates.

Formatting text
> Topics explain what options are available for making text bold, italicized, and underlined. Topics will also explain how to use color text. Use graphics to demonstrate coloring tools.

Procedural Help Topics

How to create new documents
> Topics include steps for creating new documents. There will also be procedures for selecting templates.

How to use formatting tools
> Topics include steps for using the bold, italicize, and underline buttons. There will also be steps for using the text-coloring feature.

Multimedia
> Use multimedia clip for each overview topic. Store and access clips off of CD-ROM.

Creating new documents
> Clip demonstrates using a template. Clip to be approximately 30 seconds long.

Formatting text
> Clip demonstrates using formatting tools. Clip to be approximately 45 seconds long.

Figure 3-1. A help project outline

simulate working with the application while you simulate providing online help based on the topics in your outline.

Whatever means you use to test the outline, your goal is the same. By testing your outline, you are making sure it covers the information needed by your audience. If you find there are holes in your outline, you can go back and fix the outline before you use it to schedule tasks.

Scheduling Project Tasks

As with project planning in general, different help authors have different opinions on how to schedule tasks. Some help authors prefer to schedule the entire project at the beginning of project planning. Their theory is that, by scheduling at the beginning of project planning, you can add in the time necessary for planning the project itself. You will have to find a style that works best for you, but I don't think you can accurately schedule a project until you know the topics and features the online help system will contain. You won't know this information until the end of your project planning. I therefore present information based on scheduling tasks at the end of project planning.

Different help authors also have different opinions on how you should allocate time for tasks. I've heard some theories that state you should take the total time for all of the tasks and multiply it by a number, such as 1.5 or 2, to account for unknowns that may come up during the project. Again, you have to find a system that works for you, but I don't believe in multiplying times by arbitrary numbers. Instead, I believe you should predetermine the different setbacks you might face during the project and account for them in your schedule. In general, you should consider the following issues when setting a task schedule:

Time required to write and edit help topics, create images, develop multimedia files, and create any other supporting files

These tasks should be your largest consideration. They make up the bulk of your project and therefore dictate, for the most part, how long the project will take. Many help authors use a formula to determine the amount of time it takes to research, write, and edit each topic in a HelpSet. They usually calculate approximately four hours per conceptual or procedural help topic and approximately one hour per field-level help topic. Using a formula like this is acceptable to calculate an estimate when you have no other information with which to plan, but you must remember that this is only an estimate.

The more intimate you are with your software and the more aware you are of the tasks required to develop the HelpSet (such as creating images and multimedia), the more accurately you can calculate the number of hours for each help component.

Number of personnel working on the online help project and their experience levels

Your project may or may not proceed more quickly if you have more people working on it. You must also consider the experience level of the people working on the project. Having experts for each type of component (such as images and multimedia) increases the speed of development. On the other hand, using interns or entry-level personnel can decrease the speed of development.

Time required to learn new software

If you plan to use new software to write help topics, create images, create multimedia clips, or perform other tasks, you must keep in mind the time needed to learn the new software. As you become familiar with JavaHelp, you will notice an improvement in development time. You also should consider the time spent to troubleshoot problems or contact customer support if you must resolve issues with the new software.

Time to test the finished online help system

You must build in time for testing the online help system and its components. The amount of time you estimate for this task depends on your resources. Some companies have quality-assurance personnel who are experts at testing software. Other companies require help authors to test their own systems. When you plan for testing, be sure to account for all components of the help system, such as the navigation components and multimedia clips. You will probably be more successful if you schedule testing concurrently with development.

Time to integrate the online help system with the software application

Once you have a functioning help system, you have to connect it to the software application. This process can be time-consuming; it depends on the presentation option you choose. If you include a single button to launch a standalone Help Viewer, it won't take much time to make the connection. However, when developing context-sensitive help, you must include the time it takes to assign each help topic to a specific object within the application.

Deadlines set by project leaders or other team members

Often, help authors are not allocated enough time to develop a good help system. Project deadlines and other project-related constraints pose certain obstacles to scheduling. In such cases, you must determine which tasks you are willing to sacrifice and settle for whatever help system you can best create in the limited time.

Planning Tasks Specific to JavaHelp

In addition to general project planning concepts, you must focus on tasks specific to JavaHelp development. Because of the function and features of JavaHelp, you must also consider several factors when planning your JavaHelp project.

Deciding How to Present the HelpSet

The way in which a HelpSet is presented to users—as standalone, context-sensitive, or embedded help—dictates how much extra time you need for development. During most of the development cycle, you'll access the HelpSet in a standalone manner. If your goal is to have a standalone HelpSet, you need only a mechanism for launching the JavaHelp system. In many situations, however, you have to improve usability by presenting the HelpSet as context-sensitive or embedded help.

For context-sensitive help, you must account for the time involved in assigning map IDs (from the map file) to the appropriate controls in the application. The amount of time to budget depends on how you connect the context-sensitive help. If you only connect context-sensitivity for the application's windows, it shouldn't take too much time to assign map IDs. However, if you are providing field-level help and must assign map IDs for every object and every window, you should study the application's interface to estimate the number of objects assigned map IDs.

If you are a technical writer, implementing embedded help requires close coordination with the application developer because embedded help is part of the application's interface. Discuss embedded help early during project planning, so the developer can plan for it.

Deciding How to Install the HelpSet

When you plan your JavaHelp project, you must consider how the HelpSet will be installed at the user's site. In Chapter 1, *Understanding JavaHelp*, I discussed different JavaHelp installation methods. It's important to decide on a method early enough to plan for it. You should also consider how your decision might affect the use of enhancements in your HelpSet. Earlier in this chapter, I discussed considerations for enhancing your HelpSet with images or multimedia. You must be careful with such enhancements because you don't want to frustrate your audience by making them wait for file downloads. In general, use the following guidelines for incorporating images and multimedia:

- For an independent Java application, images work well, but you should put multimedia files (depending on the number of files and their size) on a CD-ROM.

- For applets or applications that run on a local network, include images and multimedia clips on the network server.

- For applets that run in a web browser (assuming users connect with a modem), minimize the use of images. Multimedia clips are generally not feasible unless you can use *streaming*, a multimedia technology in which users can start viewing a multimedia clip before the file has completely downloaded to their computer.

Outlining the File and Directory Structure

The preceding chapter included a brief presentation of a HelpSet's file and directory structure. Since topic-to-topic links depend upon the correctness of relative

URLs, it is worth outlining the entire directory and file structure before writing individual help topics. Keep in mind that third-party help-authoring tools (discussed in Chapter 9) can help organize your project directory and file structure.

The first directory you must create is the main project directory, in which you place all other project directories and files. Name this directory after the application for which the help is written. For example, for the sample word processor application used earlier in this chapter, the main directory is named *WordProcessorHelp*. Figure 3-2 shows the directory structure for the *WordProcessorHelp* project.

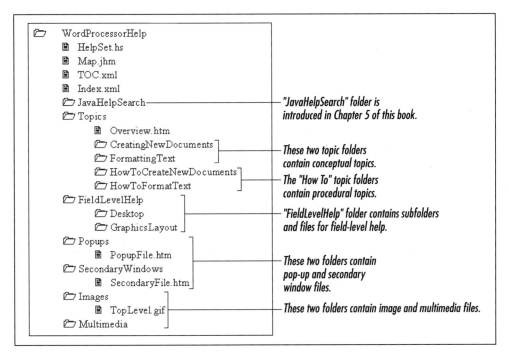

Figure 3-2. Directory and file structure for a JavaHelp project

You might use a modified directory structure if you plan to merge different HelpSets. These considerations are discussed with the information on merging HelpSets in Chapter 6, *Enhancing the HelpSet*.

Structuring HelpSet data and navigation files

When you outline your file and directory structure, keep in mind that all JavaHelp files refer to each other by their relative positions to one another:

- The HelpSet file refers to the map file and the navigation files (TOC, index, and word-search index).

- The map file refers to all the help topic HTML files.

For example, a HelpSet file might refer to the map file like this:

```
<mapref location="Map.jhm"/>
```

The filename *Map.jhm*, with no directory location, indicates that the map file is in the same directory as the HelpSet file.

I strongly suggest that you keep the HelpSet, map, and navigation files in the main project directory. The files reference each other by filename only, without having to specify any directories.

Structuring topic and field-level help directories and files

All topic directories and files are listed relative to the location of the map file. For example, the map file from the preceding chapter includes these lines:

```
<mapID target="computers" url="Topics/Interests/Computers.htm"/>
<mapID target="fitness" url="Topics/Interests/Fitness.htm"/>
```

The directory *Topics*, along with the subdirectory *Interests* and file *Computers.htm*, is listed relative to the map file: the *Topics* directory is at the same directory level as the map file.

I strongly recommend having one major *Topics* directory at the same level as the map file, as illustrated in Figure 3-2. Notice that I placed the *FieldLevelHelp* directory outside the *Topics* directory. You usually have the word-search index utility search the entire *Topics* directory to build its search database. (I discuss this utility in Chapter 5, *Creating HelpSet Data and Navigation Files.*) Excluding the field-level help files from that directory means they won't show up in any word search. If you want to include field-level help in the word-search index, place the *FieldLevelHelp* directory under the *Topics* directory. Alternatively, add the topics to the search database manually, as discussed in Chapter 6.

Structuring images and multimedia files

The main project directory should also have directories to hold any images and multimedia files. Figure 3-2 show *Images* and *Multimedia* directories. As with each of the topic directories, use these directories to store files as you develop them throughout the project.

Structuring pop-up and secondary window files

A final consideration when outlining your file and directory structure is whether or not you want the JavaHelp system to display some your HelpSet's topics in pop-up windows and secondary windows. As discussed in Chapter 6, pop-up and secondary window topics are simply HTML files, just like the rest of your topic files.

However, you should consider storing these files outside your *Topics* directory for two reasons:

- You will find it easier to stay organized if you keep pop-up and secondary window files in their own directories.

- You will probably want to exclude pop-up and secondary window topics from the word-search index.

Therefore, as with the *FieldLevelHelp* directory, you should place these directories outside of the *Topics* directory.

Planning the Navigation Components

Planning for your navigation facility depends on the size of your HelpSet and whether or not you use a third-party help-authoring tool to create it. If you use a third-party tool, the time to create the navigation facility is negligible—since the third-party tool does the work for you. If you create your HelpSet manually, you should plan on creating the navigation components as you write the online help topics. Add enough time to your schedule to add each topic to the TOC and index, keeping in mind that there will probably be several index entries for each topic. You shouldn't have to plan too much time for the word-search index, since JavaHelp includes a utility for generating it.

4

Preparing Help Topics

The two most important features of any online documentation system are well-written, meaningful topics and a good navigation facility. This chapter discusses the former.

JavaHelp topics are written in HTML. This chapter doesn't teach you HTML, but it explains how to apply HTML to certain parts of JavaHelp topics. If you are not familiar with HTML, you may want to consult O'Reilly's *HTML: The Definitive Guide.*

While most of the concepts in this chapter apply to all online documentation systems, I discuss them as they apply to JavaHelp. To help you create well-written and meaningful JavaHelp topics, this chapter provides the following guidelines for accomplishing the following tasks:

- Planning your help topics
- Creating help topics and applying appropriate HTML tags
- Writing effective and meaningful help topics
- Using preexisting HTML topic files

Planning Your Help Topics

In the previous chapter I outlined the entire JavaHelp project. I also explained that you should determine general help-topic areas based on your research of the audience and their needs. In this section I examine the following basic tasks that break down the general topic subject areas into specific online help topics:

- Assigning work to help authors
- Organizing information into help topics
- Obtaining approval from team members

Assigning Work to Help Authors

If you are working with a team of help authors, there are various methods for dividing the work among the team members. One method is to make each help author responsible for a different type of topic. For example, if three help authors were working on a project, one could work on field-level help, another on conceptual help, and the other on procedural help.

If the help authors have limited time for learning the application for which they are writing online help, you might try another method, in which each writer works in a specific subject area (such as creating new documents or formatting text). This method has each writer creating topics of all types (field-level, conceptual, and procedural) for his or her assigned subject area. The benefit to this approach is that each author spends time learning only a small portion of the application.

For large projects, you should assign the help-topic types (field-level, conceptual, procedural, etc.) to teams. Then have each team allocate help topics to the individual help authors. For example, if a team of help authors is working on field-level help, have each author work on the topics for different screens. Then, you won't have help authors duplicating efforts, and each author can remain focused on a specific type of help topic. Again, depending on your resources, you might have help authors focus on particular subject areas instead of topic types, to minimize the time required for learning the subject matter.

If you are working alone on the project, it's still wise to think of the different topic types and subject areas as separate components. Although you are responsible for everything, breaking things down can help you approach the project in an organized manner.

Organizing Information into Help Topics

Once you know the specific topic types and subject areas for which you are responsible, you can begin organizing specific information into individual help topics—a process known as *chunking*. For example, if you want to create procedural help that explains how to use the word processor's formatting tools, first determine specific procedures, such as how to embolden text, how to italicize text, and how to color text. You then place each of these procedures in a separate help topic instead of combining them in one long topic.

At this point in the project you should have an idea of the information the help topics will contain, so you can give each topic a title. Keep your project organized as you create the topic titles. In the last chapter, I used the word processor-application example to show how to organize the general help types and subject areas into a directory and file structure. When you decide on the topic titles, start creating the actual files within your directory structure. You won't write the topic content yet, but you can accomplish two tasks at once if you create the topic's HTML file at the same time you outline your topics and create topic titles. For example, you can create actual HTML files for the help topics on emboldening, italicizing, and coloring text. You aren't yet ready to write the actual content or procedures within the help topics, but you can determine their titles based on the information the topics provide. Later, when you write the content of each help topic, you can simply use the appropriate HTML file you have already created.

Based on the word processor example, Figure 4-1 shows how you might set up a directory and file structure for help topics on formatting text.

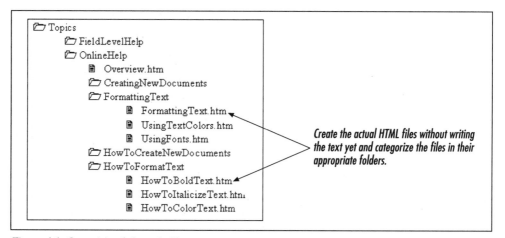

Figure 4-1. Organizing help topic files

When I outline topics for a new help project, I usually create and categorize the topic files with their actual topic titles as shown in Figure 4-1. Then, when I want to print out or show someone my outline, I simply take screen shots of the directory and file structure and use them as my printed outline.

Later in this chapter I provide some tips on chunking the individual help topics, designing topic titles, and naming topic files.

Obtaining Approval from Team Members

When you have determined the specific help topics you will prepare, you should present them to other members of your development team to get general approval. Depending on your company, this approval could be a verbal "sounds good to us," or it could be a formal proposal, requiring signatures from team members, verifying that your help topics are appropriate for the project. Make sure that everyone agrees that the topics you have outlined can be prepared by the project deadline.

If you present the report to managers, or if you are working under particular deadlines, you should include anticipated completion dates to show that you can complete the help topics in time for the project deadline. In Chapter 3, *Planning the JavaHelp Project*, I discussed determining the time required for you to create help topics.

Creating Help Topics and Applying Appropriate HTML Tags

Before you start writing the text for your help topics, you should understand the concepts behind naming the topic's HTML file, formatting text in the topic, and using links to different topics and web sites.

Naming the HTML Files

When you create your HTML files, consider the tips in this section for choosing meaningful filenames and keeping your project well organized. If you use consistent, logical filenames, you should be able to recognize the subject of the help topic just by looking at its filename.

When naming files, consider the following related HelpSet items:

- Filenames
- Map IDs
- Topic titles

Name the help-topic files in such a manner that anyone can easily match them to their corresponding map ID and topic title. However, you don't want to give the files ridiculously long names that become hard to manage. I tend to use nearly identical names for all three related items. So, for a word-processor help topic on formatting text, I would use the map ID "FormattingText," the filename "FormattingText.htm," and the topic title "Formatting Text."

NOTE   If you use a third-party help-authoring tool to create your HelpSet,
              you may not have a choice in assigning the map ID: the third-party
              tool may automatically create it. However, third-party tools that auto-
              matically assign the map ID typically allow you to work at the topic-
              title level, so that you don't have to pay attention to map IDs.

Applying Formats to Text

Before writing text for your help topics, you should know how to use HTML formatting tags in JavaHelp topics. As you write each topic, you will want to apply formatting tags to the topic title heading, subheadings, body text, bulleted lists, and
numbered lists.

In Chapter 2, *Creating Your First HelpSet*, you used HTML tags to format text within
help topics. You probably remember that it was as simple as writing a basic web
page, since the HelpSet Viewer is based on HTML. Now take a closer look at applying available formatting tags to JavaHelp topics. Figure 4-2 shows the HelpSet
Viewer with a help topic that contains a variety of text formatting.

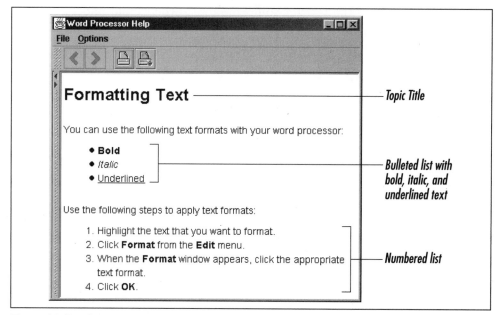

Figure 4-2. Displaying formatted text

Here is the source text for the topic shown in Figure 4-2; it uses standard HTML
formatting tags:

```
<html>
<head>
<title>Formatting Text</title>
</head>
<body>
<h1>Formatting Text</h1>
<p>You can use the following text formats with the word processor:
<ul>
  <li><strong>bold</strong></li>
  <li><em>italic</em></li>
  <li><u>underlined</u> </li>
</ul>
<p>Use the following steps to apply text formats:
<ol>
  <li>Highlight the text that you want to format.</li>
  <li>Click <strong>Format</strong> from the <strong>Edit</strong> menu.</li>
  <li>When the <strong>Format</strong> window appears, click the appropriate
      text format.</li>
  <li>Click <strong>OK</strong>.</li>
</ol>
</body>
</html>
```

This text uses the following HTML formatting tags:

- `<h1>` identifies the topic title. You can use `<h2>` and additional heading levels throughout the help topic if you want to break it down into subsections.

- `<ul>` and `<li>` identify the bulleted list.

- `<strong>` identifies bold text, `<em>` identifies italicized text, and `<u>` identifies underlined text.

- `<ol>` and `<li>` identify the numbered list.

At the time of this writing, the HelpSet Viewer doesn't support the following HTML tags or attributes:

- `<font>` tag is not reliable; you can use basic fonts, such as Times or Arial, but the HelpSet Viewer doesn't interpret all fonts.

  If you don't specify a font with the `<font>` tag, JavaHelp uses a default sans-serif font.

- `<map>` and `<img usemap>` tags (for client-side image maps).

- `<tt>` and `<code>` tags (for monospace typeface).

You should refer to JavaHelp's documentation or Sun's web site for ongoing updates to this information.

Keep in mind that you should not use a lot of text formatting in the same help topic just because you can. Too much formatting can be a strain on the reader's eyes. Reserve text formats such as bold, italics, underlines, and color for special conditions. These text formats will be more effective if you use them sparingly.

Using Links

As you create your help topics, you should consider how topics relate to one another. You might have a help topic that explains the basic concepts behind using word-processor templates and another topic that provides step-by-step procedures for using templates, but the user might not know that both of these topics exist.

You can help the user locate related topics by using HTML hyperlinks. You created a hyperlink in Chapter 2 that enabled the user to click selected text and jump to the related help topic. Creating a hyperlink is easy; you use HTML code within your help topic as demonstrated in the following example:

```
This online help system also provides conceptual information on
<a href="../UsingTemplates.htm">using templates</a>.
```

In this example, `<a href="../UsingTemplates.htm">` sets up the hyperlink so that the user can simply click the text "using templates" to jump to the related topic.

When using this kind of link, be careful selecting text to which you apply the hyperlink; you don't want to select more text than necessary. In the previous example I applied the link only to "using templates" instead of to the entire phrase "conceptual information on using templates." The latter would have disturbed the smooth flow for readers not interested in the hyperlink.

Don't use too many hyperlinks in one help topic. By following too many hyperlinks, users risk getting lost in your help system and may become frustrated enough to stop using it. Also, make sure the hyperlink actually links to a topic that expands on the subject. I have seen many cases where authors include hyperlinks that send the user to another topic, only for the user to find that the new topic doesn't actually provide additional information on the subject.

Another way to help your users is to have a "Related Topics" or "See Also" section at the bottom of the help topic. This section provides a list of other topics in the current HelpSet (or in a wider scope) that are related to the topic the user is currently reading. To make effective use of related topics, make a note of which help topics closely relate to others while you are organizing and writing the help topics.

Your audience uses related topics in a different manner than they use other hyperlinks. They turn to related topics specifically to see what other help topics exist that might help them find more information on the current topic. Since you don't force the related topics feature on users (you place it at the bottom of the help topic) you can include all topics that relate to the current one—even if you already included the topic earlier in a hyperlink.

Writing Effective and Meaningful Help Topics

No book can make you an expert on information design, and while the purpose of this book is to teach you how to develop JavaHelp projects, I also provide some tips in this section to help you prepare better JavaHelp topics:

TIP   If you are already experienced with designing help topics, you might
                   want to skip the rest of this chapter.

Understanding How Users Read Online Help

The best way to start this discussion is to explain the way users don't read online help. They don't read online help the way you are reading this book. With online help, the user doesn't read the document from start to finish. There is neither a beginning nor an end to the document.

Generally, users enter a help system with a question for which they want an answer or a task for which they need instructions. Users are typically in the middle of working with the application and don't want to spend time reading through a lot of information. They tend to skip over sections and skim through sections to find the specific information they need.

The troubling fact about online help is that you don't have many chances to give users what they want. Typically, users will try only a few times to find the information they want before giving up on finding the topic. After several futile attempts with the same help system, users start to lose faith in the information the help system provides. If you don't carefully craft the help topics, as well as the navigational facility that gets the users to the topics, you could very well waste time developing a help system that no one uses. The solution, however, is *not* to omit the help system, afraid of wasting valuable time. Instead, the solution is to take the time to create well-written and meaningful help topics through which users can find the information they need.

Chunking Information

As mentioned earlier in this chapter, when you chunk information, you are break-ing it down into separate topics so that each chunk of information treats only one subject. For examples of chunking, look through this book. You'll see that infor-mation is chunked into sections within each chapter. The previous section pro-vided information about how users read online help. This section provides infor-mation primarily about chunking.

You must be more specific when chunking information for online help than for hardcopy documents. Using the word-processor example, it's not enough to pro-vide one topic on formatting text. Instead, you need one topic that lists the types of formatting options, one topic that describes how to use bolding, one topic that explains how to use italics, and as many other topics as needed to cover all format-ting options.

Thus, Figure 4-2 may not be a good model to follow for designing a help topic. While the entire help topic discusses only text formatting, it presents multiple topic types and attempts to answer more than one question. It provides concepts on the word processor's text-formatting options and also gives procedures for for-matting the text. A good help system would have the conceptual information in one topic and the procedural information in another.

Writing the Topic Content

After you have chunked information into separate subjects, you can begin writing the topic content. Approach writing each topic as an individual document. Never assume the user has read any other help topic prior to the one you are writing. This approach means you can't assume users have any previous knowledge of the subject. Good information chunking keeps you from writing topics that require prerequisite information and therefore eliminates the tendency to write introduc-tory material in every help topic.

Most online-help users skim through information instead of reading every word and sentence. To help accommodate users' reading habits, you must write short, clear, concise sentences and use short paragraphs. You should also use small, sim-ple words. As you write each sentence and are thinking about the right words to use, remember that one important JavaHelp navigation component, the word-search index, finds topics based on the words you use within the help topic. Users type a word, and the JavaHelp index presents a list of the help topics containing that word. Therefore, try to use words you anticipate someone will use in a word search.

In addition to sentence and word structure, consider the following tips while writing your help topics:

- Avoid jargon and define all technical words and abbreviations. In Chapter 5, *Creating HelpSet Data and Navigation Files,* I discuss pop-up windows and show you how you can use them to define new words.

- If you must write a long help topic, break the topic into subheadings. Since users scan through the help topic, subheadings help them locate particular sections.

- Don't avoid writing a help topic because the subject is too confusing. Spend the time to make the subject clear and easy to understand. If a procedure in the application is difficult to document, it is probably difficult to perform. You should look at such procedures to see if you should change the actual application interface to make it easier for users.

  This tip may seem like a lot of additional work, but your users will appreciate it. The documentation phase presents an excellent opportunity to test the application's interface. Take advantage of it. Instead of trying to cover up interface flaws with awkward documentation, fix the interface so that both the application and its documentation will be friendlier to your users.

- Be consistent with your writing style and choice of words. If you refer to the software application as the "system," use this word consistently. Don't use "system" in one place, "application" in another, and "software" in another. The user will waste time trying to find the difference in meaning among these words when in fact you use them all to mean the same thing.

- Place cautions and important notes before the passage they modify. For example, if you want to tell the users that performing Step 3 will delete the contents on their hard drive, tell them before they read Step 3. Don't wait until after the user performs the action. This tip might sound obvious, but many writers place cautions like this one at the bottom of the topic or after the particular step. People won't read everything before performing a step, so make sure they know important consequences before they take action.

- Limit procedures to no more than seven steps, because users can process only about three to seven online items. If you must use more then seven steps, try breaking the procedure into multiple procedures. However, sometimes breaking procedures apart just to avoid using more than seven steps is not feasible. You are better off giving the user nine steps for a task than creating multiple procedures and making users jump through the help system to finish the task.

- Avoid using the future tense by eliminating the word "will." For example, don't say, "When you select the formatting option, the system *will* display the formatting screen." Instead say, "When you select the formatting option, the system displays the formatting screen." Users are taking action in the present tense. Making a sentence future tense by using the word "will" not only is inconsistent with the user's present action, but also makes sentences unnecessarily long and awkward.

- Write in the active voice instead of the passive voice. When you write in the active voice, you make something take action on something else instead of the "something else" being acted upon. For example, if you say, "When you select the formatting option, the system displays the formatting screen," you are using the active voice because the user takes action on the system, and the system takes action on the formatting screen. However, if you say, "The formatting screen is displayed when the formatting option is selected by the user," you are using the passive voice because the formatting screen and the formatting option are being acted upon.

  Another problem with using the passive voice is that it generally forces using a phrase such as "the user" as I did in the previous example. Since the users are the people for whom you are writing, write to them directly instead of writing about them. Use the word "you" as I did in the example of an active sentence instead of the phrase "the user" as I did in the example of a passive sentence.

Setting the Topic Length

When you are writing the help content, keep in mind the length of the help topic. There is no magical number of words per topic that will work best for your users. Setting such a number stops you from providing important information in an attempt to avoid writing longer topics. It also forces you to write longer topics in place of shorter ones just to fill up space. You must provide as much information as is required to discuss only the given subject—nothing more, nothing less.

Take a common-sense approach to setting topic length. When was the last time you enjoyed reading a lengthy topic while trying to operate a software application? Your users are most likely no different from you when it comes to reading software documentation. Give them only the information they are looking for. If doing so means writing a longer topic, your users will probably be happy that all the information they want is there. Remember, though, to break down longer help topics into subsections with their own subheadings.

Designing the Topic Title

Once you have written the topic's content, you must give the topic a title. Users should know simply by reading its title if they want to read a help topic. The topic title should tell users whether or not the help topic contains the answer to their question. For example, "Applying Bold Formatting to Text" says more to the user than "Bold Formatting."

In designing a topic title, be sure to use a short phrase that concisely describes the topic's contents. Like the topic itself, topic titles should be self-contained. Don't make a help topic title depend on text or titles from other topics. Users will see this title in JavaHelp's table of contents and must decide from there what the topic title means.

Using the <title> tags to specify the topic title

As discussed in Chapter 1, *Understanding JavaHelp*, the word-search index uses the information you place in the `<title>` tags of your help-topic files. Also, in Java-Help 1.1 and later, the titlebar of a secondary window displays the text of its topic file's `<title>` element. For this reason, you should use the topic title you speci-fied in the TOC file in your help files' `<title>` tags. For our word-processing help example, you would use the following line in the topic file to specify its title:

```
<title>Formatting text</title>
```

NOTE   It's up to you to keep the title you specify with `<title>` tags consis-tent with the topic title you specify in the TOC file.

Using Preexisting HTML Topic Files

It is quite possible that you may start a JavaHelp project with all of your HTML topic files already created. For example, you may be converting a preexisting HTML-based help system to JavaHelp, or may simply have created all your HTML topic files before beginning your JavaHelp-level work.

If you are using preexisting HTML files, rest assured that your workload for creat-ing the HelpSet will be nearly the same as if you created the HTML files specifi-cally for your HelpSet. Remember, JavaHelp uses HTML for its topic files. All you have to do is point to the HTML files in your map file. You should, however, per-form a quick check to make sure the HTML files meet the standards I discussed in this chapter. For example, you should check that your HTML files don't contain markup tags or script that the HelpSet Viewer can't interpret. You should also check that each file has a title specified with `<title>` tags, for use by JavaHelp's word-search index.

5

Creating HelpSet Data and Navigation Files

HelpSet data and navigation files connect the HTML-format help topic files of your HelpSet. To show you how to create HelpSet data and navigation files, this chapter discusses the following topics:

- Understanding XML
- Creating the HelpSet file
- Assigning map IDs to help topics
- Specifying the navigation components

Understanding XML

The JavaHelp map, TOC, index, and HelpSet files are all written in the *Extensible Markup Language* (XML). Like HTML, XML is a web standard, but it's more flexible. You can use XML to format any kind of textual data, not just web pages. In addition, you can use XML to describe the *structure* of textual data, which is how XML is used in HelpSet data and navigation files.

The map, TOC, index, and HelpSet files for the Aviation sample project contain markup tags you don't find in HTML files. For example, look at the following line from the TOC file:

```
<tocitem target="intro" text="Introduction to Aviation">
```

The `<tocitem>` tag is not a standard HTML tag. A standard web browser simply skips over this tag, but JavaHelp's HelpSet Viewer does know how to interpret it.

Each XML file contains a tree-structured hierarchy of *elements*. That is, an element can contain other elements. In particular, the *root* element of the tree contains all the other elements in the file. Elements that contain other elements have this form:

```
<tag name1="value1" name2="value2">
    text and other elements go here
</tag>
```

This kind of element has a start-tag (for example, `<tocitem ...>`), and a corresponding end-tag (for example, `</tocitem>`).

Some elements, the *leaves* of the tree structure, contain no other elements. Such elements use this single-tag form:

```
<tag name1="value1" name2="value2"/>
```

Alternatively, you can also use the separate start-tag/end-tag for such elements:

```
<tag name1="value1" name2="value2"></tag>
```

An element can have any number of "name=value" pairs, which are called *attributes*. JavaHelp makes heavy use of attributes. The value of an attribute must be enclosed in quotes. In general, you can use either single quotes or double quotes; this book uses double quotes only.

The following excerpt from the Aviation TOC file contains both kinds of elements:

```
<tocitem text="Introduction to Aviation" target="intro">
    <tocitem text="Landing Gear" target="gear"/>
</tocitem>
```

The "Introduction to Aviation" element contains the "Landing Gear" element. Accordingly, the TOC displayed by the JavaHelp system contains "Landing Gear" as a subentry of "Introduction to Aviation."

NOTE   When one or more elements are contained within another element, I use indentation to emphasize the relationship. But this is just a custom; indentation has no real meaning in an XML file. You can even place an element and its subelements on a single text line.

You may want to use comments in some of your XML files to point out information to other developers or help authors who might look at your files. An XML comment has this form:

```
<!-- text, possibly multiple lines -->
```

The comment text itself must not include a double-hyphen (--).

For example, if you want to identify a section in the map file that contains map IDs for images, place the following line just before the actual image map IDs:

```
<!-- Map IDs for Images -->
```

Creating the HelpSet File

Take a look at the HelpSet file for the Aviation JavaHelp sample. I like to keep file-names simple, so I named it *HelpSet.hs*. Another good name would be *Aviation.hs*. Regardless of what you name the HelpSet file, you must use the *.hs* filename extension; the HelpSet Viewer won't open it otherwise.

Using a text editor, open the file *HelpSet.hs*. It contains the following code:

```xml
<?xml version='1.0' encoding='ISO-8859-1' ?>
<!DOCTYPE helpset
    PUBLIC "-//Sun Microsystems Inc.//DTD JavaHelp HelpSet Version 1.0//EN"
           "http://java.sun.com/products/javahelp/helpset_1_0.dtd">

<helpset version="1.0">
  <title>Aviation Information</title>
  <maps>
    <homeID>intro</homeID>
    <mapref location="Map.jhm"/>
  </maps>
  <view>
    <name>TOC</name>
    <label>Aviation TOC</label>
    <type>javax.help.TOCView</type>
    <data>TOC.xml</data>
  </view>
  <view>
    <name>Index</name>
    <label>Aviation Index</label>
    <type>javax.help.IndexView</type>
    <data>Index.xml</data>
  </view>
  <view>
    <name>Search</name>
    <label>Aviation Word Search</label>
    <type>javax.help.SearchView</type>
  <data engine="com.sun.java.help.search.DefaultSearchEngine">
      JavaHelpSearch
    </data>
  </view>
</helpset>
```

This code demonstrates both HelpSet data tags and navigation component tags. I explain how to use tags to merge HelpSets in Chapter 6, *Enhancing the HelpSet*.

Understanding the HelpSet Data Elements

The HelpSet file begins with two optional declarations. The XML declaration (<?xml ...) and the document type definition, or DTD (<!DOCTYPE ...),

identify this file as an XML document with a particular structure. This can be use-ful if an XML-aware program other than the HelpSet Viewer needs to access the data in this file.

The HelpSet file must contain an element hierarchy whose root element is named "helpset." Accordingly, there is a `<helpset>` start-tag at the top of the file and a `</helpset>` end-tag at the bottom. You can include an optional `version` attribute in the start-tag, to specify the version of this online help project.

Within the `<helpset>` element, you create:

HelpSet data elements
> A `<title>` element and a `<maps>` element

Navigation elements
> One or more `<view>` elements

The data elements are described in the following paragraphs, and the navigation elements in the next section.

The `<title>` element specifies the name of the HelpSet, which appears in the HelpSet Viewer's titlebar:

```
<title>Aviation Information</title>
```

The `<maps>` element uses two subelements to specify essential data:

```
<maps>
  <mapref location="Map.jhm"/>
  <homeID>intro</homeID>
</maps>
```

The `<mapref>` element uses a `location` attribute to specify the location of the map file relative to the HelpSet file. The `<homeID>` specifies the map ID of the topic to be displayed when the JavaHelp system starts.

The JavaHelp system uses the data in the map file to convert map IDs into URLs. For example, the map ID `intro`, specified in the `<homeID>` element, maps to URL *Topics/introduction_to_aviation.htm.* This is the HTML file that contains the help topic "Introduction to Aviation." Thus, when the JavaHelp system first opens the Aviation HelpSet, it displays the "Introduction to Aviation" topic.

NOTE   Since you code the map ID as the contents of the `<homeID>` ele-ment, not as an attribute value, you don't have to place the map ID (`intro`) inside quotes.

Understanding the Navigation Component Elements

Following the HelpSet data elements are the navigation component elements, coded as `<view>` elements. Each `<view>` element specifies one of the navigation components: TOC, index, and word-search index. The following subelements within the `<view>` element supply the details:

- `<name>` provides an internal identifier for the navigation component. It produces nothing visible in the HelpSet Viewer. As always, I use simple names:

  ```
  <name>TOC</name>
  ```

- `<label>` specifies the text that appears in the tool tip label when the cursor rests over one of the navigation component tabs in the navigation pane of the HelpSet Viewer. For example, the following line generates the text `Aviation TOC` in the TOC tool tip label:

  ```
  <label>Aviation TOC</label>
  ```

  To see this label, run the Aviation JavaHelp sample. Point and hold the cursor over the TOC, index, and word-search index tabs.

- `<type>` provides internal information to the JavaHelp system, to specify the paths to the navigator Java class.

- `<data>` specifies the location, relative to the HelpSet file, of the file or directory that contains the data for the navigation component. For example, the data that defines the index for the Aviation HelpSet is in file *Index.xml.*

For the word-search index, the `engine` attribute specifies the search engine Java class.

Assigning Map IDs to Help Topics

The map file associates each help-topic map ID with the URL of a help topic HTML file. The map ID acts as a nickname for the file; the TOC file, index file, and word-search index file all use these nicknames to specify help topics.

In Chapter 1, *Understanding JavaHelp,* I showed you how a map file works within a HelpSet. In this section I expand on the map file by explaining how you create, edit, and structure it.

The Map File

Take a look at the map file, *Map.jhm,* for the Aviation JavaHelp sample. A portion of the contents are shown here:

```
<?xml version='1.0' encoding='ISO-8859-1' ?>
<!DOCTYPE map
```

```
    PUBLIC "-//Sun Microsystems Inc.//DTD JavaHelp Map Version 1.0//EN"
          "http://java.sun.com/products/javahelp/map_1_0.dtd">

<map version="1.0">
  <mapID target="toplevelfolder" url="Images/toplevel.gif"/>
  <mapID target="intro" url="Topics/introduction_to_aviation.htm"/>
  <mapID target="aerodynamics" url="Topics/Aerodynamics/aerodynamics.htm"/>
  <mapID target="drag" url="Topics/Aerodynamics/drag.htm"/>
  <mapID target="lift" url="Topics/Aerodynamics/lift.htm"/>
  <mapID target="thrust" url="Topics/Aerodynamics/thrust.htm"/>
  <mapID target="weight" url="Topics/Aerodynamics/weight.htm"/>
</map>
```

As in the HelpSet file, the XML declaration (<?xml ...) and the document type
definition (<!DOCTYPE ...) are optional. The root element of the map file is
named "map," specified with the <map> and </map> tags. The <map> start-tag
includes an optional version attribute, where you can specify the JavaHelp map-
version number.

The <map> element contains a series of <mapID> elements, each of which defines
one map ID. A map ID can be associated with a topic file or with an image file.

Following is a typical <mapID> element:

```
    <mapID target="intro" url="Topics/introduction_to_aviation.htm"/>
```

<mapID> elements contain no text data, just attributes. The target attribute spec-
ifies the map ID. The url attribute specifies the URL of the topic file or image file
relative to the location of the map file. In specifying the url value, be sure to:

• Separate directory names with forward slashes (/).

• Begin the URL with a character other than forward slash, because the URL
  must be *relative* to the map file.

• Include the filename extension (for example, *.htm, .html, .jpg*).

Naming the Map File

When it introduced JavaHelp, Sun used the *.jhm* filename extension on map files.
Some third-party help-authoring tools have adopted this convention. You can use
any filename extension on a map file (for example, you might want to use *Map.xml*
instead of *Map.jhm*). Just be sure that the name of your map file is specified accurately in the <mapref> element in the HelpSet file. For example:

```
    <mapref location="Map.xml"/>
```

Structuring the Map File

When you create the map file, you should understand how to structure it to make it easier to work with. You can place the map IDs in any order in the map file, but you should use a strategy that keeps your JavaHelp project well organized. In previous chapters, I discussed separating HTML files into different directories based on the subject matter of the help topics. I suggest using a similar approach with the map file. Group related topics together in the map file, and separate each group by spaces or XML comments. It doesn't matter to JavaHelp how the map IDs are organized, but it will matter to you later if you try to locate certain map IDs but can't figure out where in the map file you placed them.

I usually put images and miscellaneous map IDs at the beginning of my map file, and I put pop-up and secondary-window map IDs at the end. In the Aviation Java-Help sample map file, the first `<mapID>` element specifies a map ID for the top-level folder image. Shown in Figure 5-1, the top-level folder image appears at the top of the TOC. TOC image files are the only image files for which you must set a map ID. (I discuss other TOC image files in Chapter 6.) The top-level image file in this example is referenced only by the TOC file. You can substitute any image for it, but I recommend using the top-level folder image Sun supplies with JavaHelp.

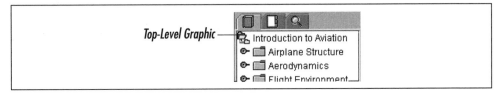

Figure 5-1. Top-level folder image

NOTE   You may want to refer back to Chapter 2, *Creating Your First HelpSet*, where I discuss working with the top-level image file.

If you use images within help topics to launch pop-up windows and secondary windows, you may also want to define them in the map file. I discuss this topic more in Chapter 6.

After the map IDs for the image files, I list the map IDs for each help topic. Notice that I separate them into related subjects and separate each set with a space. Again, you don't have to place the map IDs in any particular order, but it helps if you organize them in a recognizable pattern (for example, the same way the TOC is organized).

Try to use map IDs that are meaningful. You could simply use numbers for each ID; JavaHelp doesn't care what you use. But if you use numbers, you can't identify the content of a topic by looking at its map ID. My map IDs usually contain some or all of the help topic's HTML filename. For example, I use the map ID aerodynamics for the HTML file *aerodynamics.htm*, and I use the map ID gear for the HTML file *landing_gear.htm*.

If you are creating a very large HelpSet, you may want to create a simulated map ID hierarchy, using multipart names. For example, I could assign the map ID aircraft.gear to the HTML file *landing_gear.htm* and the map ID aircraft. wing to the HTML file *wing.htm*. Then, whenever I notice a map ID starting with "aircraft," I would know that the topic has to do with aircraft structure. Similarly, to identify map IDs for images, I use img. with the map ID. For pop-up and secondary-window topic map IDs, I use pop. and sec. respectively.

Specifying the Navigation Components

The navigation components are an important part of an effective online help system. If users can't find the information for which they need help, they will lose faith in the help system. One disappointing fact is that users won't give your navigation system many chances to prove itself. Users generally search for a help topic only a few times before they give up on finding it.

This section provides some tips on creating an effective navigation facility. Its focus, however, is to show you how to specify the various JavaHelp navigation components: the TOC, index, and word-search index.

Creating the Table of Contents

A HelpSet's TOC should function the same way as a traditional book's TOC. Users look in the TOC to find topics arranged by subject matter.

If you have been following my practices for planning a JavaHelp project, you are off to a good start planning a well-designed TOC. In discussing project planning and preparing topics in previous chapters, I encouraged you to group related subjects within their own directories to keep them organized. You can now use this same structure to present the TOC for your HelpSet. Since you already organized the directories and topic files by subject, simply mimic that structure in the TOC. The only difference is that, in the TOC, you should not necessarily alphabetize the topics within a directory. Organize the topics in a logical order according the concepts the users must know and procedures they must perform.

When placing topic titles in the TOC, be sure to use the same title that you used in the topic file's <title> element. When users select a topic from the TOC, they expect the title to be the same in the topic file. If you use the title "Landing an Airplane" in the TOC, users will be confused if the actual topic title says "Landing Gear."

Building the JavaHelp TOC

Let's take a look at the TOC file, *TOC.xml*, for the Aviation JavaHelp sample. Here is a complete listing:

```xml
<?xml version='1.0' encoding='ISO-8859-1' ?>
<!DOCTYPE toc
   PUBLIC "-//Sun Microsystems Inc.//DTD JavaHelp TOC Version 1.0//EN"
          "http://java.sun.com/products/javahelp/toc_1_0.dtd">

<toc version="1.0">
<tocitem image="img.toplevelfolder" target="intro"
         text="Introduction to Aviation">
   <tocitem target="structure" text="Airplane Structure">
     <tocitem target="empennage" text="Empennage"/>
     <tocitem target="fuselage" text="Fuselage"/>
     <tocitem target="gear" text="Landing Gear"/>
     <tocitem target="powerplant" text="Powerplant"/>
     <tocitem target="wing" text="Wing"/>
   </tocitem>
   <tocitem target="aerodynamics" text="Aerodynamics">
     <tocitem target="lift" text="Lift"/>
     <tocitem target="weight" text="Weight"/>
     <tocitem target="thrust" text="Thrust"/>
     <tocitem target="drag" text="Drag"/>
   </tocitem>
   <tocitem text="Flight Environment">
     <tocitem target="airports" text="Airports">
       <tocitem target="wind" text="Wind Direction Indicators"/>
         <tocitem target="runtaxi" text="Runways and Taxiways">
           <tocitem target="runways" text="Runways"/>
           <tocitem target="taxiways" text="Taxiways"/>
           <tocitem target="markings" text="Markings"/>
         </tocitem>
     </tocitem>
   </tocitem>
</tocitem>
</toc>
```

Figure 5-2 shows the TOC as it appears in the HelpSet Viewer.

Creating the TOC elements

As in the HelpSet file, the XML declaration (<?xml ...) and the document type definition (<!DOCTYPE ...) are optional. The root element of the TOC file is named "toc," specified with the <toc> and </toc> tags. The <toc> start-tag includes an optional version attribute, where you can specify the JavaHelp map version number.

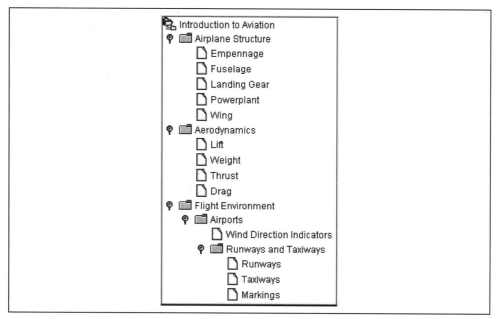

Figure 5-2. Aviation TOC

The `<toc>` element contains a set of `<tocitem>` elements. Each `<tocitem>` element uses attributes to specify one TOC entry. For example:

```
<tocitem target="intro" text="Introduction to Aviation"/>
```

In this example, when the user clicks the TOC entry "Introduction to Aviation," the topic with map ID "intro" appears. You can use these attributes in the `<tocitem>` tag:

- The `text` attribute specifies the character string to appear as the TOC entry.

- The `target` attribute specifies the map ID of the topic to be displayed when the user clicks the TOC entry. This attribute is optional; if you omit it, nothing happens when the user clicks on the TOC entry.

- The `image` attribute (not included in the above example) specifies the icon to be displayed along with the TOC entry. If you omit this attribute, the HelpSet Viewer displays an open/close control (for entries that have subentries) or a sheet-of-paper icon (for entries without subentries). Figure 5-2 shows these icons.

Creating help topic categories

When you have a group of related topics, you should create a separate category (TOC level) for them to make them easier for users to find. (I also suggest that you place the topic files in a separate directory within your help project's *Topics* directory.)

You create multiple categories by nesting <tocitem> elements within each other. For example, the following excerpt from the Aviation TOC file defines the category entry "Aerodynamics," along with subentry topics titled "Lift," "Weight," "Thrust," and "Drag."

```
<tocitem target="aerodynamics" text="Aerodynamics">
  <tocitem target="lift" text="Lift"/>
  <tocitem target="weight" text="Weight"/>
  <tocitem target="thrust" text="Thrust"/>
  <tocitem target="drag" text="Drag"/>
</tocitem>
```

NOTE   If a <tocitem> element defines a category (that is, if it has subentries), use the start-tag/end-tag form <tocitem>...</tocitem>. If a <tocitem> element defines a TOC entry with no subentries, you can use the single-tag form <tocitem.../>.

The user can open and close a category—make its subentries appear and disappear from the TOC display—by using the control that appears in front of the category entry. Figure 5-3 demonstrates this control.

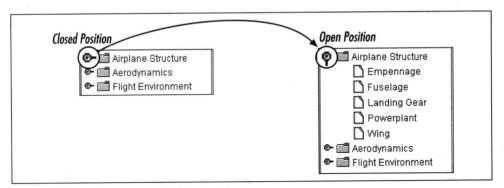

Figure 5-3. Opening and closing TOC categories

Figure 5-4 shows a more elaborate TOC entry hierarchy with a more complex nesting of categories and topics.

The <tocitem> elements that define this structure are nested in the same way:

```
<tocitem text="Flight Environment">
  <tocitem target="airports" text="Airports">
    <tocitem target="wind" text="Wind Direction Indicators"/>
    <tocitem target="runtaxi" text="Runways and Taxiways">
      <tocitem target="runways" text="Runways"/>
```

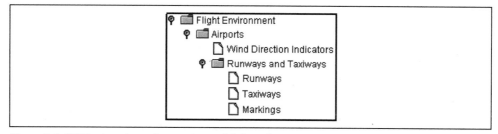

Figure 5-4. TOC categories, subcategories, and help topics

```
          <tocitem target="taxiways" text="Taxiways"/>
          <tocitem target="markings" text="Markings"/>
        </tocitem>
      </tocitem>
    </tocitem>
```

If this nesting of XML elements is confusing, just keep the nesting to a minimum.

Help topics for category entries

A TOC entry that defines a category can also have a topic associated with it. (Not all online help systems work this way.) For example, look again at the definition of the "Aerodynamics" category:

```
    <tocitem target="aerodynamics" text="Aerodynamics">
```

When the user clicks on the TOC entry "Aerodynamics," the help topic with map ID "aerodynamics" appears. If you did not want this TOC entry to link to a help topic, omit the `target` attribute:

```
    <tocitem text="Aerodynamics">
```

With this change, nothing happens when the user clicks on the TOC entry "Aerodynamics."

I recommend having a topic for every TOC entry, including categories. The most important thing, however, is to be consistent. If one category has a topic, all categories should have topics.

Creating a top-level TOC entry

You should create a top-level category to contain all other topics in the HelpSet. This entry provides an overall title for the HelpSet. Thus, the overall structure of the TOC file looks like this (using the Aviation example):

```
<toc>
<tocitem image="img.toplevelfolder" target="intro"
        text="Introduction to Aviation">
```

```
      (all other <tocitem> elements, defining help topics
      and help topic categories)

  </tocitem>
  </toc>
```

Use the `image` attribute to specify an icon to be displayed for this top-level category. Sun supplies a standard icon for this purpose, in file *toplevel.gif.* It depicts a folder containing other folders: a top-level folder (see Figure 5-1). The map file for the Aviation HelpSet assigns map ID `img.toplevelfolder` to this icon file. Accordingly, the `image` attribute in the example above uses this map ID.

The `target` attribute specifies map ID `intro`. When the user clicks the top-level item in the TOC, the HelpSet Viewer displays the introductory help topic, which is assigned to that map ID. As always, the value of the `text` attribute specifies the title to appear in the TOC—in this example, `Introduction to Aviation`.

There is no open/close control for the top-level category. The user can open or close the category by double-clicking it.

Creating the Index

Designing a good index differs from designing a good TOC because users use an index in a much different way than they use a TOC. In constructing a TOC, you organize related topics into categories. With an index, however, you focus on each topic individually. The only time you consider how multiple topics fit together is when you have to organize related secondary index items under a primary index item.

To index a topic you must first identify the main ideas associated with that topic. You may even want to record this information in a simple text file. If you want a more sophisticated approach to indexing, you can create a spreadsheet or database to store your index information. Once you have determined a topic's main ideas, you need to decide on words or short phrases that identify that topic's subject. These words and phrases should be either nouns or gerund phrases—phrases that act as nouns, usually by adding "ing" to the phrases' verbs. An example of a gerund phrase is "landing an airplane." The entire phrase acts as a noun. In this example, the gerund phrase represents the act of landing an airplane.

When you create the index, try to think of as many synonyms for your index items as possible. You have no way of knowing what word or phrase your readers are thinking of when trying to find a particular topic. One reader might look for the word "airport" while another reader might look for "landing field." Be prepared to create several index items for each help topic. Approaching the index from the viewpoints of different users is challenging, but it improves the usability of the index.

Index items are arranged alphabetically and are not capitalized unless they are proper nouns (for example, the name of a window or control). Within this alphabetized list, certain index items might contain secondary index items. For example, a primary index item may be the word "airplane." However, this item may have several nested secondary items such as "single engine," "multiple engine," "mechanics," or "about." Don't use more than two levels of index items; it's confusing to your readers and could render the index useless.

Building the JavaHelp index

Let's take a look at the index file for the Aviation JavaHelp sample, *Index.xml*:

```
<?xml version='1.0' encoding='ISO-8859-1' ?>
<!DOCTYPE index
    PUBLIC "-//Sun Microsystems Inc.//DTD JavaHelp Index Version 1.0//EN"
           "http://java.sun.com/products/javahelp/index_1_0.dtd">

<index version="1.0">
  <indexitem target="aerodynamics" text="aerodynamics"/>
  <indexitem text="airplane structure">
    <indexitem target="empennage" text="empennage"/>
    <indexitem target="fuselage" text="fuselage"/>
    <indexitem target="gear" text="landing gear"/>
    <indexitem target="powerplant" text="powerplant"/>
    <indexitem target="wing" text="wing"/>
  </indexitem>
  <indexitem target="airports" text="airports"/>
  <indexitem target="drag" text="drag"/>
  <indexitem text="four forces">
    <indexitem target="drag" text="drag"/>
    <indexitem target="lift" text="lift"/>
    <indexitem target="thrust" text="thrust"/>
    <indexitem target="weight" text="weight"/>
  </indexitem>
  <indexitem target="empennage" text="empennage"/>
  <indexitem target="powerplant" text="engine"/>
  <indexitem target="environment" text="environment, flight"/>
  <indexitem target="environment" text="flight environment"/>
  <indexitem target="fuselage" text="fuselage"/>
  <indexitem target="gear" text="gear, landing"/>
  <indexitem target="wind" text="indicators, wind"/>
  <indexitem target="intro" text="introduction"/>
  <indexitem target="airports" text="landing field"/>
  <indexitem target="gear" text="landing gear"/>
  <indexitem target="lift" text="lift"/>
  <indexitem target="markings" text="markings, runway and taxiway"/>
  <indexitem target="intro" text="overview"/>
  <indexitem target="powerplant" text="powerplant"/>
  <indexitem target="markings" text="runway markings"/>
  <indexitem target="runways" text="runways"/>
```

```
   <indexitem text="structure, airplane">
     <indexitem target="empennage" text="empennage"/>
     <indexitem target="fuselage" text="fuselage"/>
     <indexitem target="gear" text="landing gear"/>
     <indexitem target="powerplant" text="powerplant"/>
     <indexitem target="wing" text="wing"/>
   </indexitem>
   <indexitem target="empennage" text="tail"/>
   <indexitem target="taxiways" text="taxiway markings"/>
   <indexitem target="taxiways" text="taxiways"/>
   <indexitem target="thrust" text="thrust"/>
   <indexitem target="weight" text="weight"/>
   <indexitem target="wind" text="wind indicators"/>
   <indexitem target="wing" text="wing"/>
</index>
```

The structure of the index file is almost identical to that of the TOC file but with different element names. The XML declaration (<?xml ...) and the document type definition (<!DOCTYPE ...) are optional. The root element of the index file is named "index," specified with the <index> and </index> tags. The <index> start-tag includes an optional version attribute, where you can specify the Java-Help map version number.

The <index> element contains a set of <indexitem> elements. Each <indexitem> element uses attributes to specify one TOC entry. For example:

```
   <indexitem target="intro" text="introduction"/>
```

This defines the index entry introduction. When the user selects this entry, the HelpSet Viewer displays the topic with map ID intro.

The code for the Aviation JavaHelp sample index creates the index shown in Figure 5-5.

Notice that some secondary index items are nested within primary items. For example, the following code shows how five index items are nested under the primary item airplane structure:

```
   <indexitem text="airplane structure">
     <indexitem target="empennage" text="empennage"/>
     <indexitem target="fuselage" text="fuselage"/>
     <indexitem target="gear" text="landing gear"/>
     <indexitem target="powerplant" text="powerplant"/>
     <indexitem target="wing" text="wing"/>
   </indexitem>
```

The first line, which defines the primary index item, doesn't contain a target attribute to link to a help topic. It is customary for an index item not to link to a help topic if it contains subitems. In this example, if you want to associate an overview help topic for airplane structure, you can create a secondary index item and

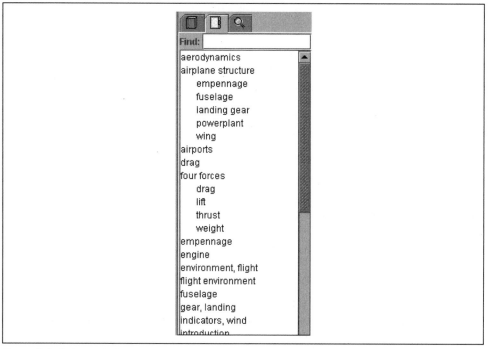

Figure 5-5. Aviation index

give it an overview name such as "about." The "about" index item provides the link to the overall airplane-structure help topic.

Notice that all the index items are alphabetized by their primary index item. In turn, any secondary index items are alphabetized within their corresponding primary item. JavaHelp doesn't alphabetize these items automatically. You must be sure to arrange the items in alphabetical order when creating the index file.

Creating the Word-Search Index

The word-search index is the most complex JavaHelp navigation component. But it is the easiest to create, since JavaHelp includes commands for automatically generating it. Creating the word-search index can be as simple as running these commands to create the default JavaHelp search index. However, you may want to take advantage of advanced features, such as hooking up another Java-based search engine to perform word-search functions.

The *jhindexer* command generates a word-search database. *jhindexer* searches all the files in the directory you specify and generates a database using the words it finds in these files. When the user enters a word-search request, the JavaHelp system looks in the database to determine the topic files in which the word or phrase is used.

Try using the *jhindexer* command to create a new word-search database for the Aviation HelpSet. Using a Unix shell window or a DOS command prompt window:

1. Go to directory *Aviation*, the master project directory for the Aviation project.

2. Delete or rename the *JavaHelpSearch* directory.

3. Enter this command to run *jhindexer* against the files in the *Topics* directory:

   ```
   C:\jh1.1\javahelp\bin\jhindexer Topics   (Windows)
   ```

   or:

   ```
   /jh1.1/javahelp/bin/jhindexer Topics   (Unix)
   ```

   These examples assume that you installed JavaHelp in directory *C:\jh1.1* (Windows) or */jh1.1* (Unix).

4. View the Aviation HelpSet in the HelpSet Viewer to see the search index that you created.

jhindexer creates subdirectory *JavaHelpSearch* in current directory, populating it with the database files that make up your HelpSet's word-search index.

WARNING   Don't change the name of any file in the *JavaHelpSearch* directory.

The directory name *JavaHelpSearch* is also specified in the HelpSet file. It's the contents of the `<data>` element within the "Search" `<view>` element. (See the listing in the previous section, "Creating the HelpSet File.") You can change the directory name and the HelpSet file specification, but I strongly recommend you don't.

You entered the *jhindexer* command with a single argument, specifying the *Topics* directory. The indexer recursively descends through the *Topics* directory hierarchy, searching the files and adding words to the word-search database. This is exactly the data that is appropriate to search: all the help topic files, but none of the image files or HelpSet data and navigation files. The convenience of having the indexer recursively descend through a single directory hierarchy is one of the reasons I strongly suggest placing all your topic files and subdirectories under one *Topics* directory.

NOTE   As discussed in Chapter 4, *Preparing Help Topics*, the word-search
                index uses the information you place in the `<title>` tags of your
                help topic files to assign names to the search results returned to a
                user conducting a search.

The *jhindexer* command offers several advanced options, which are discussed in Chapter 6.

6

Enhancing the HelpSet

So far, you have learned how to create a basic HelpSet. With the information from the previous chapters, you can create a fully functional help system with help topics, a TOC, an index, and a word-search index. You may, however, want to enhance your HelpSet by adding advanced controls within your help topics or by customizing the navigation facility.

This chapter covers the following topics that will help enhance your HelpSet:

- Creating pop-up and secondary windows
- Customizing the navigation facility
- Merging HelpSets

Creating Pop-up and Secondary Windows

You can add pop-up and secondary windows to your HelpSet for many different reasons. You might use a pop-up window to define a word within a help topic or to provide expanded information for a procedure. A secondary window is similar to a pop-up window except it provides longer and more detailed information to supplement the original help topic. The user launches a pop-up or secondary window by clicking the text, image, or button that has an encoded link to that pop-up or secondary window.

A pop-up or secondary window displays a help topic, stored in an HTML-format file. That is, the topic has essentially the same format as the "main" help topics you've seen in the preceding chapters. You can add text, images, and links to the pop-up or secondary window text. However, keep in mind the customary usage of pop-up windows (for example, to define a word in the help topic), and limit them to displaying text and images.

Differences Between Pop-up and Secondary Windows

Pop-up and secondary windows are similar, but there are some differences. Consider the following points when deciding which kind of window to use in a particular situation:

- Pop-up windows always appear directly adjacent to the object the user clicks to display them. But you can specify where secondary windows appear on the screen.

- Users can't adjust or move pop-up windows. But they can minimize, maximize, resize, and move secondary windows.

- Pop-up windows don't have titlebars: they are simply windows containing text. In JavaHelp 1.1 and later, a secondary window does have a titlebar; it displays the text of its topic file's `<title>` element.

- Pop-up windows close automatically when the user clicks another area in the HelpSet viewer. Users close secondary windows manually, by clicking the title bar's close-window button.

Even though pop-up and secondary windows are functionally different, you program them nearly the same way.

Programming Pop-up and Secondary Windows

To specify a pop-up or secondary window at some location within a help topic, you define a link using the HTML element `<object>`. The attribute `classid` specifies that the link launches a pop-up or secondary window:

```
<object classid="java:com.sun.java.help.impl.JHSecondaryViewer">
```

Nested within this element are `<param>` tags that provide the details: the link text, the kind of window to be launched, the topic to be displayed in the window, and so on.

For example, the following code from the Aviation topic file *markings.htm* defines a link to a secondary window:

```
<p>Markings provide special information for pilots when they are taxiing,
taking off, and landing. There are two types of markings:

<ul>
  <li>
  <object classid="java:com.sun.java.help.impl.JHSecondaryViewer">
    <param name="viewerActivator" value="javax.help.LinkLabel">
    <param name="viewerStyle" value="javax.help.SecondaryWindow">
    <param name="viewerLocation" value="400,200">
    <param name="viewerSize" value="600,300">
```

```
      <param name="text" value="Runway markings">
      <param name="textFontSize" value="medium">
      <param name="textFontWeight" value="plain">
      <param name="id" value="sec.runwaymarkings">
    </object>
    </li>
  ...
```

The link is defined by all the code between the <object> and </object> tags. The <p>, <ul>, and <li> tags are part of the *markings.htm* help topic containing the link: a paragraph introduces a bulleted list, which contains the text that links to the secondary window. The link text, "Runway Markings", is specified as the text parameter within the <object> element.

The parameters of the link can appear in any order within the <object> element. Each <param> tag uses name and value attributes to specify one parameter setting. For example, it might set the parameter named textFontSize to the value medium.

Several of the link object's parameters specify Java classes. (So does the object's classid attribute.) The following sections discuss these parameters.

Specifying the form of the link

The viewerActivator parameter indicates how the link appears to the user: as a button, as a text string, or as an image.

Linking with a button. A button is a quick and obvious way to set up a link to a pop-up or secondary window. To specify a button link, set the viewerActivator parameter to the value javax.help.LinkButton:

```
<param name="viewerActivator" value="javax.help.LinkButton">
```

By default, the button displays a right angle-bracket (>). You can specify the character string to appear on the button with the text parameter. For example:

```
<param name="text" value="JavaHelp Note">
```

Avoid using a long button string, which results in a large, awkward-looking button. You can format the button string, using a variety of text-formatting parameters, as described in the next section.

Linking with a text string. If you are inserting the link in a sentence, or if you simply don't want to use a button for the link, you can use inline text to represent the link to the pop-up or secondary window. For example:

```
<param name="viewerActivator" value="javax.help.LinkLabel">
<param name="text" value="Taxiway markings">
```

You can format text using font properties (family, weight, style, and size) and color. The following example shows the text-formatting parameter names in bold:

```
<param name="viewerActivator" value="javax.help.LinkLabel">
<param name="text" value="Taxiway markings">
<param name="textFontFamily" value="serif">
<param name="textFontWeight" value="bold">
<param name="textFontStyle" value="italic">
<param name="textFontSize" value="medium">
<param name="textColor" value="red">
```

Table 6-1 lists the recognized values for these text-formatting parameters. If you are accustomed to formatting text strings in HTML documents, this table should look familiar. The default value for each parameter is indicated in bold. Typically, you want your text link to stand out. Therefore, use a color such as blue to represent a link.

NOTE   This table applies both to links that are text strings (javax.help.
            LinkLabel) and to links that are button strings (javax.help.
            LinkButton).

Table 6-1. Text-Formatting Parameters

Parameter Name	Recognized Values	Comments
textFontFamily	Serif **SansSerif** Monospaced Dialog DialogInput Symbol	
textFontWeight	**plain** bold	
textFontStyle	**plain** italic	
textFontSize	xx-small (equiv: 0) x-small (1) **small (2)** medium (3) large (4) x-large (5) xx-large (6)	Absolute font-size levels, defined by the HelpSet Viewer.
	$n$pt (n is an integer)	Absolute font size, expressed in points (12 pts = 1 inch).
	+n (n is an integer) bigger means +1	Increases the font size by n font-size levels.

Table 6-1. Text-Formatting Parameters (continued)

Parameter Name	Recognized Values	Comments
	-n (*n* is an integer) smaller means −1	Decreases the font size by *n* font-size levels.
textColor	**black** **blue** cyan darkGray gray green lightGray magenta orange pink red white yellow	black is the default for a button string; blue is the default for a text string.

Linking with an image. Sometimes a button or inline text might be too plain for your needs. You can use an image as the link to the pop-up or secondary window. You can place the image inline with the text, or you can place it on a button.

An inline image link is coded similarly to a text link; just use an `iconByID` parameter instead of a `text` parameter:

```
<param name="viewerActivator" value="javax.help.LinkLabel">
<param name="iconByID" value="img.structurepic">
```

The value of the `iconByID` parameter must be a valid map ID of an image file, defined in the map file.

To place the image on a button, change the `viewerActivator` parameter value to use the `LinkButton` Java class instead of the `LinkLabel` class. (There is no `LinkImage` class in JavaHelp.)

Whether it's inline or on a button, an image can be specified by URL, instead of by map ID:

```
<param name="viewerActivator" value="javax.help.LinkLabel">
<param name="iconByName" value="../../images/forces.jpg">
```

You set the `iconByName` parameter, instead of the `iconByID` parameter. The URL specified as the value must be relative to the topic file in which the link occurs. I recommend using map IDs, since you use them for other files in your project and consistency reduces errors. Also, if you later move or rename the image files, you have to make the update only once—in the map file.

Defining the window's properties

When the user clicks on the link (text, button, or image), JavaHelp launches a pop-up window or a secondary window, depending on the value of the `viewerStyle` parameter: `javax.help.popup` or `javax.help.Secondary-Window`. For example:

```
<object CLASSID="java:com.sun.java.help.impl.JHSecondaryViewer">
    <param name="viewerActivator" value="javax.help.LinkLabel">
    <param name="viewerStyle" value="javax.help.Popup">
```

Pop-up and secondary windows permit different types of customization. You can define only the size of a pop-up window, but you can define the size, location, and name of a secondary window.

To specify the size of a pop-up or secondary window, you set the `viewerSize` parameter:

```
<param name="viewerSize" value="300,125">
```

This example specifies a window that is 300 pixels wide and 125 pixels high.

Setting the appropriate window size is mostly a trial-and-error process. After you set the window's size, run the help system and try the link to see if the topic fits in the pop-up or secondary window. If the window is too small, a scroll bar appears to enable scrolling through the entire window. Whenever possible, I prefer to set the window size so that the pop-up or secondary topic fits without the need for scroll bars.

Since a pop-up window automatically appears directly adjacent to the object the user clicks to display it, you can't define its location. You can, however, set the secondary window's location, using the `viewerLocation` parameter:

```
<param name="viewerLocation" value="400,200">
```

This example places the secondary window's upper-left corner 400 pixels from the left edge of the screen and 200 pixels down from the top edge.

A pop-up window automatically closes when the user clicks outside it. A secondary window stays open, though, until the user manually closes it.

By default, the JavaHelp system ensures that only one secondary window is open at a time. If the user clicks a link that launches a secondary window, any currently open secondary window closes automatically.

You can implement the multiple-windows strategy with *viewer names*. The link that defines a secondary window can have a `viewerName` parameter:

```
<param name="viewerName" value="MoreInfo">
```

More precisely, the JavaHelp system now ensures that only one secondary window *with a given viewer name* is open at a time. But the user can have a `MoreInfo` secondary window open, along with a `GlossaryTerm` secondary window and a `TipOfTheDay` secondary window.

NOTE   I don't recommend using the viewer names feature. If the user can open any number of secondary windows, navigation can easily become a nightmare.

Viewer names would be more useful if you could define properties only once, for all secondary windows with the same name. But unfortunately, all `<object>` links are independent, even if they have the same `viewerName` settings.

You can experiment with viewer names by modifying the secondary window links in the Aviation topic files. Use different names for the `value` attribute to see if the secondary windows remain open. Make backup copies of the original Aviation topic files before you start, so that you can restore the originals when you're done experimenting.

Keep in mind that certain properties that may seem like window properties are actually set in the HTML file used for the pop-up or secondary window. For example, the background color of a secondary window is in fact the background color of the topic. You'd therefore define the color directly in that topic's HTML file.

Defining the window's content

When JavaHelp opens the pop-up or secondary window, it displays the topic you specify with the `id` parameter:

```
<param name="id" value="pop.jhhelpid">
```

The value of the `id` parameter must be a valid map ID of a topic file, defined in the map file.

Alternatively, you can specify the URL of the topic file using a `content` parameter instead of an `id` parameter:

```
<param name="content" value="../../pop-ups/fourforces.htm">
```

The URL you specify as the value must be relative to the current topic file. As with image links, I recommend using map IDs, not URLs.

Customizing the Navigation Facility

The navigation facility is one of the most important features of any help system. Without it, users can't find the information they need. Because the navigation facility is so important, you may want to customize it to fulfill your users' needs. You can customize the navigation facility in many different ways.

Changing Navigation Components' Tool Tips

One feature that is easy to customize is the navigation components' tool tips. The user sees these tool tips when the cursor rests over any of the navigation tabs in the HelpSet Viewer's navigation pane. For example, when the cursor rests over the Aviation HelpSet's TOC tab, a tool tip pops up with the name **Aviation TOC**. The tool tips work the same way for the index and word-search index tabs, as well.

You can change the tool tips by modifying the contents of the `<label>` elements for each navigation component specified in the HelpSet file. Give it a try:

1. Open the Aviation HelpSet file (*HelpSet.hs*) in a text editor.

2. Modify the TOC tool tip by changing the following line in the TOC section:

   ```
   <label>Aviation TOC</label>
   ```

   to:

   ```
   <label>Table of Contents</label>
   ```

3. Modify the index tool tip by changing the following line in the index section:

   ```
   <label>Aviation Index</label>
   ```

   to:

   ```
   <label>Alphabetical Index</label>
   ```

4. Modify the word-search index tool tip by changing the following line in the word-search index section:

   ```
   <label>Aviation Word Search</label>
   ```

   to:

   ```
   <label>Word Search Index</label>
   ```

5. Save the HelpSet file and load the Aviation HelpSet into the HelpSet Viewer.

When the help system opens, pause the cursor over each navigation tab in the navigation pane. Note the changes in the tool tips.

Excluding Navigation Components

You can also customize the navigation components to which users have access. If for some reason you don't want to include the TOC, index, or word-search index, you can simply remove it from the HelpSet file. You may not have known it at the time, but you effectively performed this action in Chapter 2, *Creating Your First HelpSet*, when you created a simple HelpSet. You omitted the `<view>` element specifying a word-search index from the MyJavaHelp HelpSet file. The result was a HelpSet containing only the TOC and index in the navigation pane.

When you exclude a navigation component you must remove its entire `<view>` element: everything from the `<view>` start-tag to the `</view>` end-tag. Give it a try by removing the word-search index from the Aviation HelpSet:

1. Open the Aviation HelpSet file (*HelpSet.hs*) in a text editor.

2. Delete the following lines:

```
<view>
  <name>Search</name>
  <label>Aviation Word Search</label>
  <type>javax.help.SearchView</type>
  <data engine="com.sun.java.help.search.DefaultSearchEngine">
    JavaHelpSearch
  </data>
</view>
```

3. Save the HelpSet file and load the Aviation HelpSet into the HelpSet Viewer.

When the help system opens, note that there is no index tab in the navigation pane.

Rearranging Navigation Component Tabs

In each HelpSet you've seen so far in this book, the navigation pane has opened with the TOC as the active navigation component. The order of the navigation tabs, from left to right, has been the TOC tab, the index tab, and the word-search index tab.

You are not, however, limited to this navigation structure. You can change the structure to accommodate any needs you or your users might have. The most common alternative is to make the navigation pane open with the index active, instead of the TOC. This is common because users of online help systems typically know what information they are trying to find. Instead of wading through a TOC, users frequently turn to the index to find a short word or phrase that summarizes the topic for which they want information. For this reason, it might make sense for you to make the navigation pane open with the index active.

In JavaHelp, you don't specify the navigation component you want to display when a particular HelpSet loads. Instead, if you want to make the index the default navigation component, just make it the first navigation component in the HelpSet file. The order of `<view>` elements in the HelpSet file defines the order of the navigation tabs in the HelpSet Viewer.

You can experiment with this feature by modifying the Aviation HelpSet file. Using cut-and-paste, move the entire `<view>` element that defines the index above the `<view>` element that defines the TOC:

```
<helpset version="1.0">
  <title>Aviation Information</title>
  <maps>
    <mapref location="Map.jhm"/>
    <homeID>intro</homeID>
  </maps>
  <view>
    <name>Index</name>
    <label>Aviation Index</label>
    <type>javax.help.IndexView</type>
    <data>Index.xml</data>
  </view>
  <view>
    <name>TOC</name>
    <label>Aviation TOC</label>
    <type>javax.help.TOCView</type>
    <data>TOC.xml</data>
  </view>
  . . .
```

View the Aviation HelpSet. Note that the index appears first, not the TOC, and note that the order of the navigation tabs corresponds to the order of the `<view>` elements.

You can also create additional navigation tabs. What if you want to present two different TOCs—one for novice users and the other for expert users? Simply create a second TOC file and add a `<view>` element defining the other TOC to the HelpSet file. When you run the JavaHelp system, the navigation pane now contains four navigation tabs instead of the usual three.

Try this with the Aviation HelpSet. There's a file named *AnotherTOC.xml* in the main project directory. It contains only information about airplane structure. Modify the HelpSet file, adding the `<view>` element printed in bold:

```
  . . .
  <view>
    <name>TOC</name>
    <label>Aviation TOC</label>
    <type>javax.help.TOCView</type>
    <data>TOC.xml</data>
  </view>
  <view>
    <name>TOC</name>
    <label>Airplane Structure TOC</label>
    <type>javax.help.TOCView</type>
```

```
    <data>AnotherTOC.xml</data>
  </view>
  <view>
    <name>Index</name>
    <label>Aviation Index</label>
    <type>javax.help.IndexView</type>
    <data>Index.xml</data>
  </view>
  . . .
```

Note that the secondary TOC's tool tip, "Airplane Structure TOC" differs from the tool tip of the primary TOC. This helps the user understand the difference between the two TOCs. Run the Aviation JavaHelp sample, and note the changes.

Customizing the TOC

So far you have seen the icons shown in Figure 6-1 in all the TOCs you have worked with.

Figure 6-1. TOC icons

I have already explained the top-level image icon in previous chapters. It is an image you specify in both the map and TOC files, and it appears at the top of the TOC. The other two icons, the help topic category and the help topic icons, are default icons set by the HelpSet Viewer.

You can change any or all of these icons. In fact, there are a couple of situations in which you might want to change them. One situation would be if you wish to adhere to company standards that might require the same "look and feel" as older help systems. Many of these older help systems use book and page icons. Another situation might be if you want to use custom icons for different types of help topics. For example, you might want to use an image of a regular page for conceptual topics, an image of a number for step-by-step procedures, and an image of tools for troubleshooting topics.

To use a custom icon, place the image file in the project's *Images* directory and specify a map ID and URL in the map file. For example, the beginning of your map file might look like this:

```
<mapID target="img.toplevelfolder" url="Images/toplevel.gif"/>
<mapID target="img.bookicon" url="Images/category.gif"/>
<mapID target="img.pageicon" url="Images/topic.gif"/>
```

You can then add `image` attributes to `<tocitem>` elements in the TOC file, specifying the appropriate icon map IDs. For example:

```
<tocitem image="img.bookicon" target="structure" text="Airplane Structure">
  <tocitem image="img.pageicon" target="empennage" text="Empennage"/>
  <tocitem image="img.pageicon" target="fuselage" text="Fuselage"/>
</tocitem>
```

Try customizing the icons in the Aviation JavaHelp sample. Before you start, download the TOC icon files from the "Examples" section of this book's web page. Once you have the icons on your computer, use the following steps to customize the TOC:

1. Copy the three image files you downloaded from the book's web site (*toplevel. gif*, *category.gif*, and *topic.gif*) to the *Images* subdirectory of the *Aviation* project directory. The *toplevel.gif* file from the web site should replace the original *toplevel.gif* file.

2. Add the following lines to the map file:

```
<mapID target="img.bookicon" url="Images/category.gif"/>
<mapID target="img.pageicon" url="Images/topic.gif"/>
```

3. In the TOC file, add the `image` attribute along with the appropriate image map ID to each category and topic line. When you are finished, the TOC file should look like the following example:

```
<?xml version='1.0' encoding='ISO-8859-1' ?>
<!DOCTYPE toc
   PUBLIC "-//Sun Microsystems Inc.//DTD JavaHelp TOC Version 1.0//EN"
          "http://java.sun.com/products/javahelp/toc_1_0.dtd">

<toc version="1.0">
  <tocitem image="img.toplevelfolder" target="intro"
          text="Introduction to Aviation">
    <tocitem image="img.bookicon" target="structure" text="Airplane Structure">
      <tocitem image="img.pageicon" target="empennage" text="Empennage"/>
      <tocitem image="img.pageicon" target="fuselage" text="Fuselage"/>
      <tocitem image="img.pageicon" target="gear" text="Landing Gear"/>
      <tocitem image="img.pageicon" target="powerplant" text="Powerplant"/>
      <tocitem image="img.pageicon" target="wing" text="Wing"/>
    </tocitem>
    <tocitem image="img.bookicon" target="aerodynamics" text="Aerodynamics">
      <tocitem image="img.pageicon" target="lift" text="Lift"/>
    </tocitem>
    ...
```

4. Run the Aviation JavaHelp sample and note the changes. Your TOC should resemble the TOC shown in Figure 6-2.

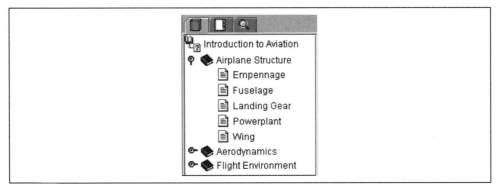

Figure 6-2. TOC with custom icons

Applying Advanced Word-Search Index Features

In Chapter 5, *Creating HelpSet Data and Navigation Files,* you learned how to create a basic word-search index. However, you are not limited to the default options you accepted when you created this search index; you can manipulate it to accommodate custom needs.

Customizing a word-search index generally means using a configuration file to modify different aspects of the search index. A configuration file is simply a text file with instructions on how the JavaHelp indexer should create the word-search index. To keep matters simple, I name my configuration file *Config.txt.*

You use the configuration file by using the –c option to the *jhindexer* command. For example, with the Aviation HelpSet, enter this command:

```
jhindexer -c Config.txt Topics
```

The rest of this section explains the different uses for the configuration file, including changing the pathnames of topic files, identifying specific topic files to index, and modifying stopwords.

Changing pathnames of topic files

You will most likely never need to change the pathnames of topic files, especially if you encapsulate your HelpSet files into a JAR file. However, at the risk of confusing you, I discuss this topic only because you might come across it in Sun Microsystems' documentation and wonder what it is about. But keep in mind that if you follow the strategies presented in this book for directory and file management, you will never have to worry about this topic.

If the path to the topic files you create during development is different from that used later by the help system to find the topic files during searches, you must use the configuration file to account for this change. For example, let's say you store your *Topics* directory (the directory containing all your help topic files) in a separate directory on your computer, away from your other HelpSet files, or on another computer on a network. Later you reassemble the help system so that the *Topics* directory is in the same directory structure as the remaining HelpSet files. You then have to provide information to the JavaHelp indexer so it can record the location of the topic files at search time.

If you deviate from my guidelines in this book and should find the need to change the path names of topic files, you can do so either by removing a portion of the pathname or by adding a portion of it to the beginning of the existing path (known as *prepending*).

Use the `IndexRemove` command in the configuration file to remove the beginning portion of the path. For example, to change the path from *Development\Documentation\OnlineHelp\MyJavaHelp* to *OnlineHelp\MyJavaHelp*, use the following `IndexRemove` command in the configuration file:

```
IndexRemove Development\Documentation\
```

If you want to add to a pathname, use the `IndexPrepend` command in the configuration file. For example, to change a path from *\MyJavaHelp* to *\OnlineHelp\MyJavaHelp*, use the following command in the configuration file:

```
IndexPrepend OnlineHelp\
```

Identifying specific topic files to index

If you want to include only certain topic files in the word-search index instead of all the files in the topic directories, you must specify these files in the configuration file. To specify the files you want to include in the word search, use the `File` command in the configuration file, as shown in this example:

```
File Topic1.htm
File Topic2.htm
File Topic3.htm
```

Be sure to place each filename on a separate line with its own `File` command.

Modifying stopwords

Stopwords are words excluded from the word-search index and not stored in the word-search database. The purpose of stopwords is to eliminate the redundancy of small, common words such as "a" or "the" in the word-search index's list of hits.

By default, the JavaHelp indexer excludes the following words from the word-search index:

a	did	his	now	than	way
all	do	how	of	that	we
am	does	if	off	the	what
an	etc	in	on	them	when
and	for	is	or	then	where
any	from	it	our	there	which
are	goes	let	own	these	who
as	got	me	see	this	why
at	had	more	set	those	will
be	has	much	shall	though	would
but	have	must	she	to	yes
by	he	my	should	too	yet
can	her	nor	so	us	you
could	him	not	some	was	

You can modify the use of stopwords in the following two ways:

- You can ignore the stopwords so that the indexer indexes every word in your help topics.

- You can specify your own custom stopwords to exclude from the word-search index.

To ignore stopwords, you don't have to use a configuration file. Instead, use the *jhindexer* command's **-nostopwords** option:

```
jhindexer -nostopwords Topics
```

To specify your own stopwords, you can use either of two methods:

- In the configuration file, include the **StopWords** command followed by a comma-separated list of stopwords:

```
StopWords a, an, the, and, but, or, nor, for, so, yet
```

- List the stop words, one per line, in a separate text file, and specify the filename in the configuration file:

```
StopWordsFile Stopwords.txt
```

    You don't have to name the stopword file *Stopwords.txt*, but this filename keeps your naming conventions simple. Save this text file in the main project directory, along with the configuration file, so that *jhindexer* can locate it.

Regardless of which method you use, when you specify your own stopwords, the JavaHelp indexer doesn't use the default stop list. The words you specify replace the default list. For this reason, you might want to use your stopwords in a text file that already contains Sun's default list. That way you have both the default list and your own custom list in one file.

NOTE   To save time typing all the default stopwords into a text file, a stop-
              word list is posted under "Examples" on this book's web page. This
              stopword list contains all of the default stopwords. You can use this
              file as a starter and add your own custom stopwords.

Combining multiple configuration commands

Each command in a configuration file must be on a separate line. For example:

```
IndexRemove Development\Documentation\
File Topic1.htm
File Topic2.htm
File Topic3.htm
StopWordsFile Stopwords.txt
```

Merging HelpSets

You can merge HelpSets so that two or more independent HelpSets appear together in the HelpSet Viewer, almost as if they were a single HelpSet. On the HelpSet Viewer's TOC navigation tab, all the HelpSets' TOCs are concatenated. Data is combined similarly on the index and word-search index tabs.

A "product suite" provides an ideal opportunity for using this facility. For each component in the suite—such as a word processor, spreadsheet application, or database application—you can develop a separate HelpSet. Then, you can merge all the HelpSets to provide a unified online help system for the entire suite.

Using the <subhelpset> Element

To merge multiple HelpSets, add one or more `<subhelpset>` elements to the HelpSet file whose data should appear first (the *master* HelpSet file). Add these elements just before the `</helpset>` end-tag, as shown in the following example:

```
<helpset>
  ...
  <subhelpset location="../OtherProject/HelpSet.hs"/>
  <subhelpset location="../ThirdProject/HelpSet.hs"/>
</helpset>
```

The `location` attribute specifies the location of another HelpSet file relative to the location of the current HelpSet file. Data from the merged HelpSets appears in the navigational controls in the order of the `<subhelpset>` elements.

The TOC navigation components to be merged must all have the same view name:

```
<view>
    <name>TOC</name>              (view name of this component is "TOC")
    ...
</view>
```

Similarly, all index views should have the same view name, and all word-search index views should have the same view name.

Try merging the MyJavaHelp HelpSet you created in Chapter 2 with the Aviation HelpSet, as follows:

1. Note the location of the *MyJavaHelp* project directory. (In this example, assume the *MyJavaHelp* directory is at the same level as the *Aviation* directory.)

2. Verify that the TOC and index navigation components have the same view name ("TOC" and "Index") in both HelpSet files.

3. In the Aviation *HelpSet.hs* file, add this line before the `</helpset>` end-tag:

   ```
   <subhelpset location="../MyJavaHelp/HelpSet.hs"/>
   ```

   You can also specify the location of a HelpSet with an absolute pathname, such as:

   ```
   <subhelpset location="/net/boron/apps/Blivet/HelpSet.hs"/>
   ```

   or:

   ```
   <subhelpset location="R:\apps\Blivet\HelpSet.hs"/>
   ```

4. Save the HelpSet file, and then view the Aviation HelpSet. Note that the navigation components are appended.

5. When you finish looking at the changes, revert to the original HelpSets from the backups you made previously.

The Drawbacks of Merging

There are a few drawbacks with merging HelpSets. Several of them result from the fact that the HelpSet Viewer simply appends navigation component data; it doesn't combine the data in a more sophisticated way.

Your TOCs appear exactly as they would if the HelpSets were not merged. If you include a top-level folder image for each TOC, the icon appears multiple times in the merged TOC—once for each TOC that originally contained the image (see Figure 6-3).

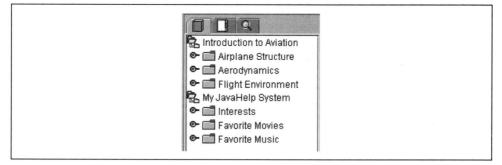

Figure 6-3. Awkwardly merged TOC

The indexes are simply appended, so even if the individual indexes are in alphabetical order, the merged index isn't. This drawback doesn't apply to the word-search index. When the user enters a word or phrase, the word-search index searches all HelpSets' databases and displays all the topic titles together.

The tool tip that appears when you rest the cursor over a navigation tab displays the text that was defined in the master HelpSet file. When you merged the MyJava-Help and Aviation HelpSets, you probably noticed that the tool tips for the tabs were **Aviation TOC**, **Aviation Index**, and **Aviation Word Search**.

In addition to limitations with the navigation controls, you are also limited by the location attribute in the <subhelpset> tag. To make the location of the secondary HelpSet file relative to the master HelpSet file, you must place the entire secondary HelpSet in a disk location adjacent to the master HelpSet file. This limitation is the reason you moved the *MyJavaHelp* directory in the previous example to merge it with the Aviation HelpSet. If the secondary HelpSet is located in a separate directory structure, you have to use an absolute location with the protocol type, as shown in the following example:

```
<subhelpset location="file:/c:/MyJavaHelp/HelpSet.hs"/>
```

The problem with using an absolute location is that if the HelpSet resides on an end user's computer, you don't necessarily know the absolute location to specify in the master HelpSet file. You then need an installation utility to determine this information and change the master HelpSet file during installation.

Overcoming the drawbacks

There are certain actions you can take to overcome most of these limitations. If you are planning a HelpSet that might later be merged with another, you should keep in mind some development alternatives.

If you don't want the top-level image to recur throughout the TOC, avoid using the top-level image in all TOC files. That way the image doesn't reappear throughout the TOC when the HelpSets are merged. For example, with the TOC in

Figure 6-3, you could eliminate the img attribute from each TOC-file line that specifies the top-level image.

The index presents problems that are difficult to resolve because there is no way to alphabetize the index items after they are merged. The best way to work around this limitation is to add a top-level index item in all merged indexes with a phrase that identifies the particular HelpSet. This mean that your index could end up with three levels of index items. For example, the index file for MyJavaHelp would resemble the following example:

```
<index version="1.0">
<indexitem text="My JavaHelp System">
  <indexitem target="computers" text="computer interests"/>
  <indexitem text="favorites">
    <indexitem target="movies" text="movies"/>
    <indexitem target="music" text="music"/>
  </indexitem>
  <indexitem target="fitness" text="fitness interests"/>
  <indexitem text="interests">
    <indexitem target="computers" text="computers"/>
    <indexitem target="fitness" text="fitness"/>
  </indexitem>
  <indexitem target="movies" text="movies, favorite"/>
  <indexitem target="music" text="music, favorite"/>
  <indexitem target="overview" text="overview"/>
</indexitem>
</index>
```

Notice that the first-level index item ("My JavaHelp System") doesn't have a target because you don't want it to launch an actual help topic. Also, notice that its tags contain the rest of the index nested within it. The biggest setback with using this approach is that the index will seem awkward if it is ever used independently (as opposed to being merged with other indexes).

Managing Projects with Merged HelpSets

Planning for a merged HelpSet begins before any HelpSet is even created. You should look at the application for which you are creating online help and decide if it offers the potential for add-on or supplemental applications. For example, if you are creating online help for a word-processing application, it's possible you may want to later merge it with other office suite products. Also, if you are creating online help for different JavaBean™ components, you should consider how HelpSets for the individual beans might eventually be merged.

The best way to keep merged HelpSets organized is to use a dataless master HelpSet file. A dataless master HelpSet file keeps all the merged HelpSets organized. It doesn't contain map or specific navigation view data for individual HelpSets. Instead it provides a container for the <subhelpset> elements that specify the HelpSet files to be merged. The following example shows a dataless master HelpSet file that merges the MyJavaHelp and Aviation HelpSets:

```
<?xml version='1.0' encoding='ISO-8859-1' ?>
<!DOCTYPE helpset
    PUBLIC "-//Sun Microsystems Inc.//DTD JavaHelp HelpSet Version 1.0//EN"
           "http://java.sun.com/products/javahelp/helpset_1_0.dtd">

<helpset version="1.0">
  <title>Merged JavaHelp System</title>
  <view>
    <name>TOC</name>
    <label>TOC</label>
    <type>javax.help.TOCView</type>
  </view>
  <view>
    <name>Index</name>
    <label>Index</label>
    <type>javax.help.IndexView</type>
  </view>
  <view>
    <name>Search</name>
    <label>Word Search</label>
    <type>javax.help.SearchView</type>
  </view>
  <subhelpset location="Aviation/HelpSet.hs"/>
  <subhelpset location="MyJavaHelp/HelpSet.hs"/>
</helpset>
```

In this example, I placed the master HelpSet file in a master project directory and placed the secondary HelpSet files in the *Aviation* and *MyJavaHelp* directories adjacent to the master *HelpSet.hs* file. The title and tool-tip labels in the master HelpSet file use generic wording so they are appropriate for any merged HelpSet. Also, the navigation view names in all HelpSet files are the same; the tool tips appear the same whether the HelpSets are viewed alone or are merged.

7

Using the JavaHelp API for Advanced Presentation Options

Throughout this book, you have viewed HelpSets in *standalone* mode, using the HelpSet Viewer utility. However, you may also need to create online help systems that work with Java applications. This chapter discusses a number of advanced presentation options—ways to tie the help system to the application:

- The TypeFacer application
- Invoking Help with a button, menu item, or key
- Using screen-level context-sensitive help
- Using field-level context-sensitive help
- Embedding help into the application

To show you the coding effort involved, this chapter works through a progressive example, showing how to connect JavaHelp to a Java application. The material assumes you are already familiar with Java programming.

I don't discuss how to create new Java components for displaying custom information in the help topics themselves. For example, you could create a multimedia object that plays movies or audio clips and then insert multimedia clips in your help topics.

While good practice dictates that you should plan online help when planning the application for which it is written, many times the application already exists and the help system is added later. Since this situation is a reality, that's where I'll start. Fortunately, adding JavaHelp after an application is developed is not a monumental task.

The TypeFacer Application

I will start with a simple application called Typeface Tester (TypeFacer for short) to illustrate the important pieces of commercial applications without confusing you with the thousands of pages of code that go into commercial applications. You can download the code for this application and its HelpSet from "Examples" on this book's web site. To execute the examples in this section:

1. Create a new directory, called *TypeFacer*, in which you'll be editing, compiling, and running Java programs.

2. Download the file *typefacer.zip* from this book's web site, placing it in the *TypeFacer* directory.

3. Unpack this ZIP file, preserving the subdirectory structure. You can use any ZIP utility, but it's easiest just to use the JAR utility:

   ```
   jar -xvf typefacer.zip
   ```

   The ZIP file contains a Java source file, *TypeFacer.java*. It also contains a subdirectory hierarchy, *TFhelp*, which in turn contains the TypeFacer application's HelpSet: HelpSet data files, navigation files, topic files, and image files.

4. Compile the TypeFacer application:

   ```
   javac TypeFacer.java
   ```

5. Run the application:

   ```
   java TypeFacer
   ```

The TypeFacer window is shown in Figure 7-1.

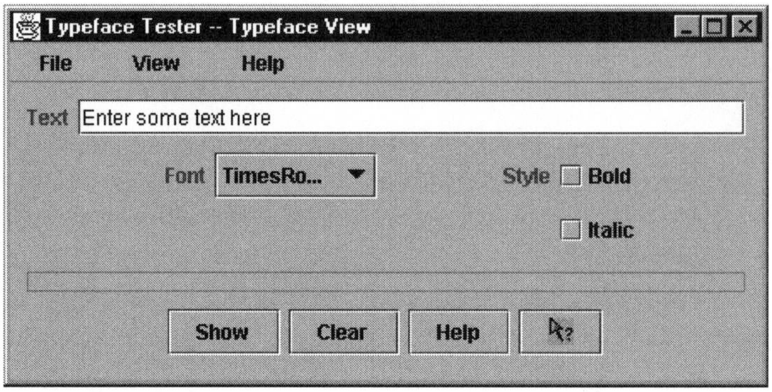

Figure 7-1. Typeface Tester application

TypeFacer enables you to select a variety of fonts, typeface styles, and colors. You can then type some sample text to see how it would look in a particular style.

The following skeleton code shows the outline of the application before we add JavaHelp-related code. (See Appendix D, *TypeFacer.java Source Listing*, for a complete listing of the application, including the JavaHelp-related code.) The application defines two screens, **Typeface View** and **Color View**, which are managed by the Java Swing `CardLayout` manager. Swing GUI components implement a menu bar, an input text field, selection buttons (for the font face, style and color), and control buttons (for showing and clearing the display). Anonymous inner classes handle the events coming from the various buttons and menu items.

Since the objective here is to add help to an application, not to learn Java programming, let's move on. If you want to know more about developing graphical Java applications, refer to O'Reilly's *Java Swing*, by Robert Eckstein, Marc Loy, and Dave Wood.

```
/*
 * TypeFacer.java
 * A simple application for styling sample text.
 */

// imports of Java class libraries
...

public class TypeFacer extends JFrame {

// data items
    // screen components
    // menu components
    // CardLayout manager setup
    // fonts and colors
    // combo box choices and titles

// constructor method

  public TypeFacer() {

  // create and size a JFrame; set up content pane

  // set up top-most panel containing text-input field

    JLabel inputLabel = new JLabel("Text");
    inputField = new JTextField("Enter some text here", 30);

  // set up middle panel, in which two cards will
  // be displayed: typefCard and colorCard

    JPanel typefCard = new JPanel(new GridLayout(2,4,5,5));
    JPanel colorCard = new JPanel(new GridLayout(2,4,5,5));
```

```java
// TypeFace card: create components

  JLabel fontLabel = new JLabel("Font", JLabel.RIGHT);
  fontChoice = new JComboBox(fontList);

  JLabel styleLabel = new JLabel("Style", JLabel.RIGHT);
  boldBox = new JCheckBox("Bold");
  italicBox = new JCheckBox("Italic");

// Colors card: create components

  JLabel foreLabel = new JLabel("Foreground", JLabel.RIGHT);
  foreChoice = new JComboBox(colorList);
  foreChoice.setSelectedIndex(0);  // initialize to "black"

  JLabel backLabel = new JLabel("Background", JLabel.RIGHT);
  backChoice = new JComboBox(colorList);
  backChoice.setSelectedIndex(5);  // initialize to "white"

// set up styled output panel

  displayField = new JTextField(40);
  displayField.setEditable(false);
  displayField.setFont(new Font("TimesRoman", Font.PLAIN, 16));
  displayField.setHorizontalAlignment(SwingConstants.CENTER);

// set up button panel

  showButton = new JButton("Show");
  clearButton = new JButton("Clear");

// set up menu structure

  fileMenu = new JMenu("File");
  exitItem = new JMenuItem("Exit");
  viewMenu = new JMenu("View");
  typeItem = new JMenuItem("Typefaces");
  colorItem = new JMenuItem("Colors");

  JMenuBar menuBar = new JMenuBar();
  menuBar.add(fileMenu);
  menuBar.add(viewMenu);

// fill the fonts and colors hashtables

// activate the buttons

  showButton.addActionListener(new ActionListener() {
    ...
```

```
        });
        ...


    // activate the menu items

      exitItem.addActionListener(new ActionListener() {
        public void actionPerformed(ActionEvent ae) {System.exit(0);}
      });
        ...
  }


  // main program: instantiate a TypeFacer object

    public static void main(String args[]) {
      (new TypeFacer()).setVisible(true);
    }
  }
```

To save space, the code listings later in this chapter show only the lines that must be added or revised in order to implement JavaHelp features.

Invoking Help with a Button, Menu Item, or Key

The simplest online help addition to any application is a menu item that starts the help system. Typically, a **Help** menu item is not context-sensitive: the help system always opens with the default help topic specified in the HelpSet file. The user can manually navigate through the TOC or search through the index or word-search index for other help topics.

Other standard ways to start the help system include clicking a **Help** button and pressing a **Help** key (by custom, function key F1). It's up to you to decide which mechanism(s) to use. Follow these steps to add all three help activators to the TypeFacer example: menu item, button, and function key. Instead of writing new lines of code, you just need to uncomment (that is, remove the comment indicators from) lines that are already there. For this revision of the program, all the lines to be uncommented start with //#1. Use your text editor's search command to locate these lines.

1. Import the Java class library for JavaHelp:

   ```
   import javax.help.*;
   ```

2. Create new instance variables for HelpSet-level classes, and for the Help menu item and Help button:

   ```
   HelpSet hs;
   HelpBroker hb;
      ...
   ```

```
JButton     helpButton;
 ...
JMenu helpMenu;
JMenuItem helpItem;
```

3. Create the Help menu item and button objects themselves:

```
helpButton = new JButton("Help");
 ...
buttonPanel.add(helpButton);
 ...
helpMenu = new JMenu("Help");
helpItem = new JMenuItem("Contents...");
helpMenu.add(helpItem);
 ...
menuBar.add(helpMenu);
```

4. Activate the Help menu item and button objects, using a convenience method from the JavaHelp API's CSH class to create an ActionListener. Programmers should familiarize themselves with this class. It contains many static helper methods, such as the DisplayHelpFromSource() method used here:

```
// activate the Help menu item and Help button

ActionListener helper = new CSH.DisplayHelpFromSource(hb);
helpItem.addActionListener(helper);
helpButton.addActionListener(helper);
```

5. Instantiate the HelpSet as a Java class, and create an associated *HelpSet broker* object (see the following description). Enable the F1 function key, specifying the topic to be displayed (this call doesn't access the HelpSet's default topic).

```
// open HelpSet, send console message
// hardcoded location: "HelpSet.hs" in "TFhelp" subdirectory

try {
  URL hsURL = new URL((new File(".")).toURL(), "TFhelp/HelpSet.hs");
  hs = new HelpSet(null, hsURL);
  System.out.println("Found help set at " + hsURL);
}
catch (Exception ee) {
  System.out.println("HelpSet not found");
  System.exit(0);
}

// create HelpBroker from HelpSet
hb = hs.createHelpBroker();

// enable function key F1
hb.enableHelpKey(getRootPane(), "overview", hs);
```

6. Compile the revised TypeFacer source file:

```
javac TypeFacer.java
```

The application now relies on JavaHelp support. Accordingly, the compilation will fail if you haven't placed the JavaHelp JAR file, *jh.jar*, on your Java class path.

7. Run the application:

```
java TypeFacer
```

8. Figure 7-2 shows the resulting Help menu.

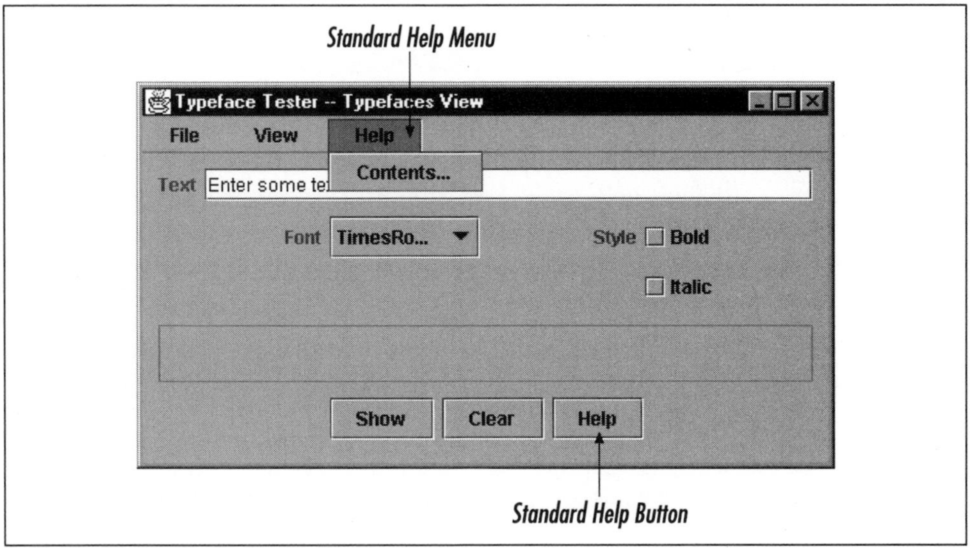

Figure 7-2. A help menu and help button

The code in Step 5 specifies the HelpSet from which to instantiate a Java `HelpSet` object. In this example, the HelpSet is stored in file *HelpSet.hs*, located in a subdirectory, *TFhelp*, of the TypeFacer application directory:

```
URL hsURL = new URL((new File(".")).toURL(), "TFhelp/HelpSet.hs");
```

Alternatively, you could retrieve the HelpSet from a web server:

```
URL hsURL = new URL("http://your.server.com/TFhelp/HelpSet.hs");
```

Or the HelpSet might be encapsulated in a local or remote JAR file:

```
URL("jar:http://your.server.com/jars/TFhelp.jar!/HelpSet.hs");
```

(For more on JAR files, see Chapter 8, *Deploying the Help System to Your Users.*)

The code creates a HelpSet broker (`HelpBroker`) object for the HelpSet. The broker handles communication between the application and the help system. Java-Help programmers should get to know the broker interface well. It handles all the retrieval and manipulation of HelpSet properties (all of the `get()` and `set()` methods are here). You can find out what entry is currently being displayed or you can enable help for a particular component. While the example in this section doesn't use the `HelpBroker` extensively, you'll notice that you must pass it as an argument to many of the other parts in our application. All those other objects rely on the `HelpBroker` to manage the help system. Essentially, this interface is how your application plays with the HelpSets you create.

Using Screen-Level Context-Sensitive Help

You should now have a TypeFacer application in which the user can open the HelpSet Viewer to a default help topic. You can enhance the help system by using *screen-level context-sensitive help*. You need to program the help system to know the user's current location within the application. The help system then displays a relevant topic when the user calls for help.

The TypeFacer application has two screens through which the user sets text and background properties. Figure 7-3 shows these Typeface View and Color View screens.

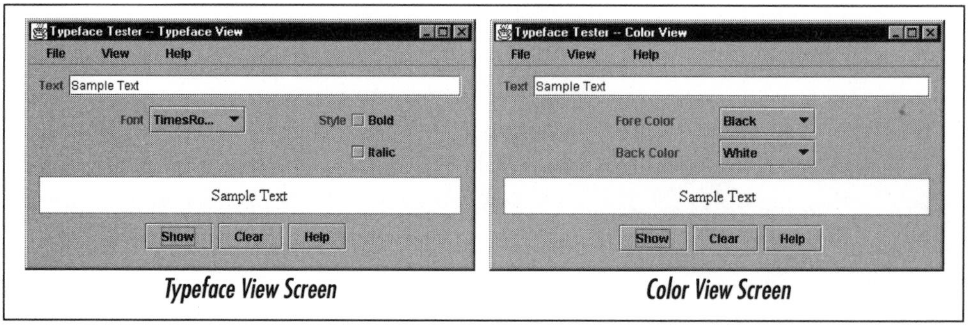

Figure 7-3. Typeface Tester's two screens

Other applications might have similar modes (for example, "edit mode" and "outline mode") or might have separate screens for different application tasks. Either way, the active mode or screen serves as a good indicator of which help topics the user might need. Rather than starting with the HelpSet's default help topic, you can go directly to the help topic for the active mode or screen.

Programming Screen-Level Context-Sensitive Help

Programming context-sensitive help is straightforward using the JavaHelp API's
CSH (context-sensitive help) class. You don't change how the HelpSet is loaded;
you simply connect a help topic to each combination of a screen context (Typefaces screen or Colors screen) and a help activator (menu item, button, or function key).

Use the following steps to make these specifications. For this revision of the program, all the lines to be uncommented start with //#2.

1. Update the `ActionListener` for the **Typefaces** menu item:

```
// configure function key F1, help button, help menu item
CSH.setHelpIDString(TypeFacer.this.getRootPane(), "typefaces");
CSH.setHelpIDString(helpItem, "typefaces");
CSH.setHelpIDString(helpButton, "typefaces");
```

2. Update the `ActionListener` for the **Colors** menu item:

```
// configure function key F1, help button, help menu item
CSH.setHelpIDString(TypeFacer.this.getRootPane(), "colors");
CSH.setHelpIDString(helpItem, "colors");
CSH.setHelpIDString(helpButton, "colors");
```

3. Compile (*javac*) and run (*java*) the revised TypeFacer application.

The `CSH.setHelpIDString()` method assigns a particular help topic to a user-
interface component—in this example, to an entire screen (that is, to function key
F1), to a menu item, or to a button. This method takes two arguments: the component and the help topic's map ID as specified in the map file.

Now, when users are at the Typeface View screen, they can view the help topic with
map ID `typefaces` by clicking the **Help** button, or by clicking the **Help** menu, or
by pressing the F1 function key (see Figure 7-4).

Similarly, when users are at the Color View screen, they see the help topic in
Figure 7-5.

Keeping an Overview Help Topic

You may have noticed a slight bug in the implementation of screen-level context-
sensitive help: now that the menu item **Contents** is context-sensitive, it doesn't provide access to the HelpSet's overview topic. Typically, a help menu with multiple
help items meets this need. Figure 7-6 shows a screen in which the user can access
the overview help topic or a help topic for the current screen.

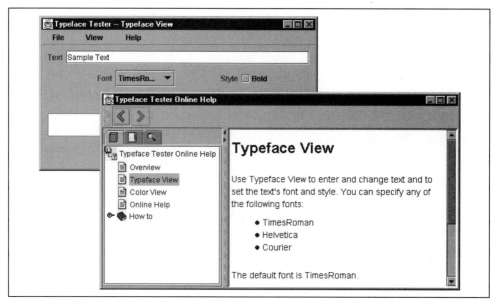

Figure 7-4. Context-sensitive help for the Typeface View screen

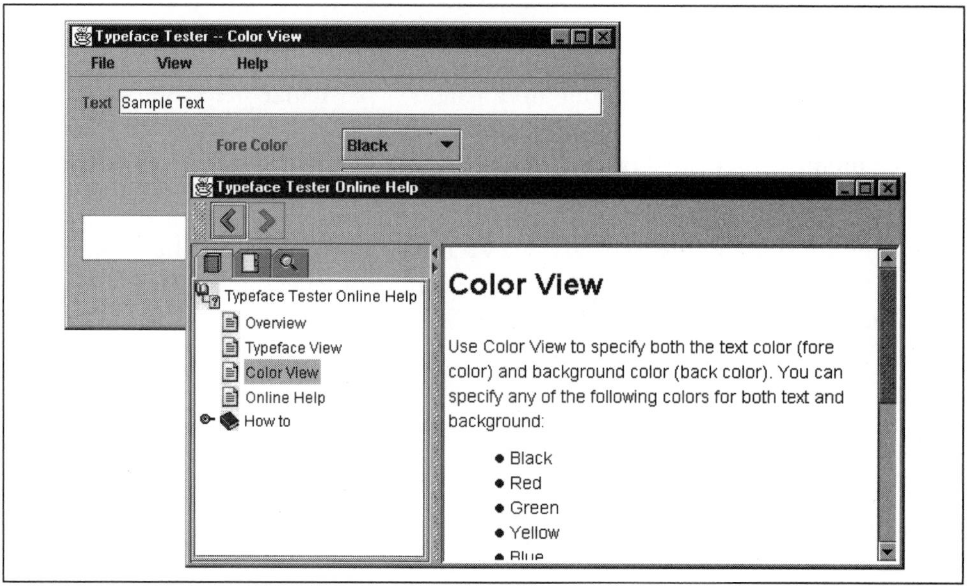

Figure 7-5. Context-sensitive help for the Color View screen

Use the following steps to set up the **Contents** menu item to launch the help system, loading the HelpSet and displaying the overview topic. For this revision of the program, all the lines to be uncommented start with //#3.

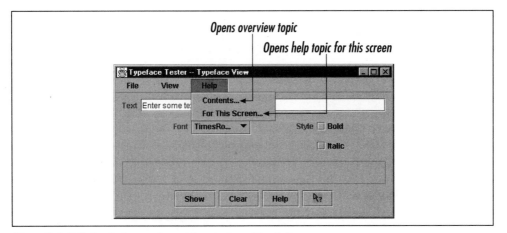

Figure 7-6. Offering both overview and context-sensitive help

1. Create a new menu item, set its associated help topic, and activate it with the same `ActionListener` you used for the **Help** button:

```
JMenuItem helpItemTOC;
  ...
helpItemTOC = new JMenuItem("Contents");
helpMenu.add(helpItemTOC);
CSH.setHelpIDString(helpItemTOC, "overview";
  ...
helpItemTOC.addActionListener(helper);
```

2. Change the wording of the existing menu item (so that you don't have two menu "Contents" items!):

```
helpItem = new JMenuItem("Contents...");
  ... change to
helpItem = new JMenuItem("For This Screen...");
```

3. Compile (*javac*) and run (*java*) the revised TypeFacer application.

Now users can choose which way they want to open the HelpSet: at an overview topic or at a topic for the current context.

Using Field-Level Context-Sensitive Help

You can take context-sensitivity one step further and implement *field-level help* (sometimes called What's This? help). In this scheme, the user clicks a button or selects a menu item that causes the mouse pointer to change—perhaps to a question mark. The user then clicks a control, such as a button or selection box, and the application displays online help specific to that control.

The TypeFacer application consists of buttons, boxes, and text-display areas, all of which are potential targets for field-level help. For example, a user might not know what the **Show** button does—a situation perfect for using field-level help. Figure 7-7 shows the help system after a user accesses field-level help for the **Show** button.

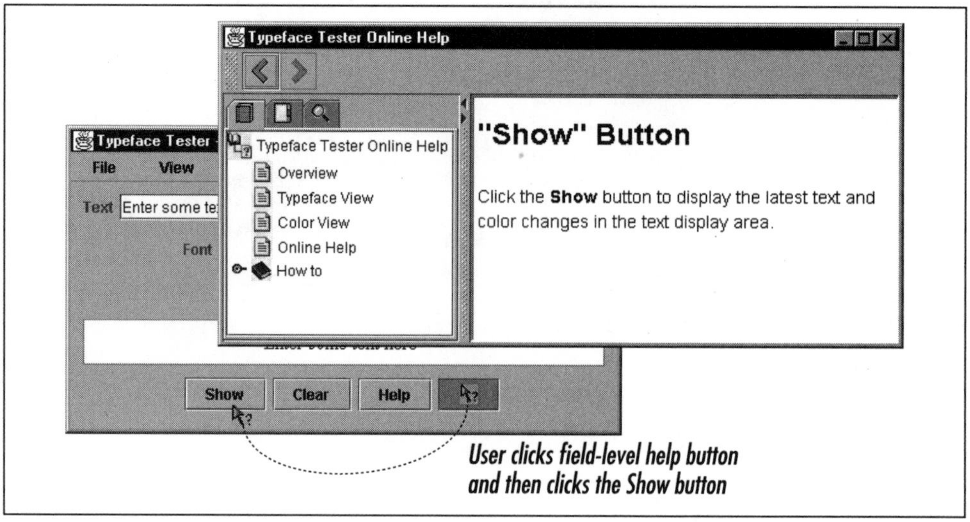

Figure 7-7. Field-level help

Programming Field-Level Context-Sensitive Help

Field-level context-sensitive help works like screen-level context-sensitive help. You use the same setHelpIDString() method as for screen-level help. Using this method, you provide a map ID for every component in the application, not just its usage modes or screens.

Use the following steps to add field-level context-sensitive help to the TypeFacer application. For this revision of the program, all the lines to be uncommented start with //#4.

1. Associate a help topic with each user-interface component:

```
// assign map IDs for field-level context-sensitive help

CSH.setHelpIDString(inputField, "text");
CSH.setHelpIDString(fontChoice, "font");
CSH.setHelpIDString(boldBox, "bold");
CSH.setHelpIDString(italicBox, "italic");
CSH.setHelpIDString(showButton, "view");
CSH.setHelpIDString(clearButton, "clear");
CSH.setHelpIDString(helpButton, "help");
CSH.setHelpIDString(qButton, "whats_this");
CSH.setHelpIDString(displayField, "text_display");
CSH.setHelpIDString(foreChoice, "fore_color");
CSH.setHelpIDString(backChoice, "back_color");
```

2. Create a button for field-level help. (Make your own *help.gif* image or download the one at this book's web site. In any case, place the image file in the *TypeFacer* directory.)

```
JButton qButton;
  ...
qButton = new JButton(new ImageIcon("help.gif"));
  ...
buttonPanel.add(qButton);
```

3. Enable the field-level help button, using another convenience method in the CSH class:

```
qButton.addActionListener(new CSH.DisplayHelpAfterTracking(hb));
```

4. Compile (*javac*) and run (*java*) the revised TypeFacer application.

The `DisplayHelpAfterTracking()` method creates a handler that tracks the mouse movement after the user clicks the field-level help button. When the user selects a user-interface component, the method activates the help system, displaying the topic associated with the component. And all this takes just a single line of code!

If your application needs more control than this handler provides, look at the source code for the CSH class itself. It defines an inner class for supporting field-level help, which can serve as a good starting point for writing your own handler.

Embedding Help into the Application

To maximize the availability of help information, consider embedding online help into your application. Rather than running the HelpSet Viewer in a separate window (and a separate operating system process), you can place the JavaHelp content pane and navigation pane directly into your application window. Chapter 1, *Understanding JavaHelp*, provides a conceptual explanation of embedded help in more detail.

When embedding help, you can retrieve and arrange JavaHelp components as you do text areas and buttons, which gives you the greatest amount of control over the JavaHelp system. However, it can also increase programming requirements, depending on how responsive to user actions the help system must be.

Understanding Embedded Help

The JavaHelp API contains methods for handling the separate parts of the HelpSet Viewer individually:

• The HelpSet Viewer's content pane displays the help topics (HTML files). In the JavaHelp API, the content pane is known as a *content viewer*.

- The navigation pane typically includes three tabs, each providing a way to find and display help topics. In the JavaHelp API, these tabbed navigation components are known as *navigators*.

Thus, you can associate a number of different navigators with a single viewer. This modularity enables you to create customized (and often impressive) help viewers for your application. You can also create custom navigators and attach them to existing viewers.

Once you decide which JavaHelp components you want to use, you can retrieve them and then add them to standard Java containers. Figure 7-8 shows an example of embedded help in the TypeFacer application.

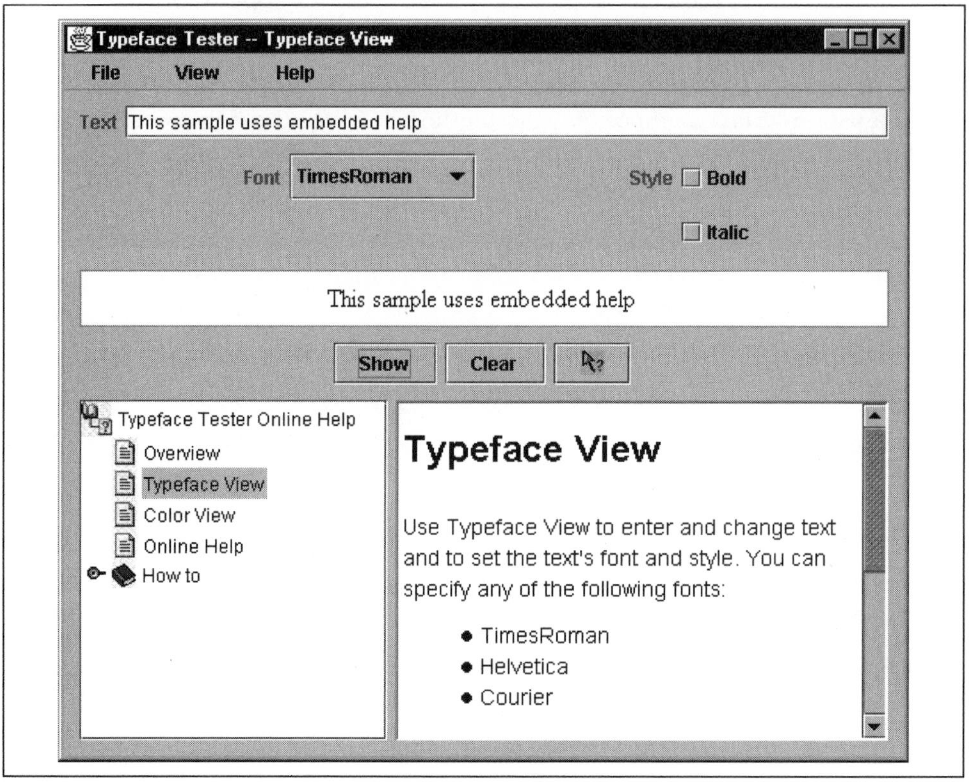

Figure 7-8. Embedded help

Programming Embedded Help

Use the following steps to implement embedded help. For this revision of the program, all the lines to be uncommented start with //#5.

1. Create instance variables for the embedded-help user-interface components:

```
// Instance variable for the Embedded Help pieces
JPanel helpPanel;
JHelpNavigator nav;
JHelpContentViewer viewer;
```

2. Change the size of the TypeFacer window to accommodate the embedded help panel:

```
setSize(500, 500);
```

3. Add a panel that contains a viewer subpanel and a navigator (TOC) subpanel:

```
// create an embedded help panel
helpPanel = new JPanel(new GridLayout(1,2,5,5));
//helpPanel.add(displayPanel);

// add a content viewer
viewer = new JHelpContentViewer(hs);
viewer.setPreferredSize(new Dimension(200,220));

// add a navigator with a table of contents view
nav = (JHelpNavigator)
    hs.getNavigatorView("TOC").createNavigator(viewer.getModel());
nav.setPreferredSize(new Dimension(200,220));

// add the components to the layout
helpPanel.add(nav);
helpPanel.add(viewer);
contentPane.add(helpPanel);
```

4. Compile (*javac*) and run (*java*) the revised TypeFacer application.

The JHelpNavigator and JHelpContentViewer components you use here are the same components the HelpSet Viewer uses. They are part of the javax.help package, so no extra imports are required. If your HelpSet's topic are extensively cross-linked, the content viewer might be all you need. Most likely, though, you will want to set up one or more navigators in addition to the content viewer.

The getNavigatorView() method provides access to the views defined in your HelpSet file; you specify the view by its name: TOC, Index, or Search. This method returns an instance of the NavigatorView class, which is the base class for building navigator objects. You can use this class to create a navigator user-interface component for the view. The createNavigator() method instantiates such a navigator object; the viewer.getModel() argument ties the new navigator to the content viewer you just created. Now when the user selects an entry from the TOC, the viewer displays the corresponding help topic.

Programmatic Control of the Viewer Topic

In this section, you'll add context sensitivity to the TypeFacer application's embedded help:

- You'll make the embedded help system initially display the topic (`typefaces`) that matches the application's initial screen (the Typefaces screen).

- You'll have embedded help automatically switch to the appropriate help topic as the user switches between the Typefaces and Colors screens.

The technique is similar to the one used in the previous section "Programming Screen-Level Context-Sensitive Help." I don't recommend implementing context-sensitivity at the field level instead of the screen level. The increased "flashing" can be disconcerting for the user.

You'll also enhance the application to enable users to hide the embedded help panel if it becomes distracting.

Implementing context sensitivity

Use the following steps to set TypeFacer's initial embedded-help topic and automatically change the help topic as the user switches between TypeFacer's two screens. For this revision of the program, all the lines to be uncommented start with `//#6`.

1. Set the initial help topic:

```
viewer.setCurrentID("typefaces");
```

2. Establish screen-level context sensitivity by updating the event handlers for the **Typefaces** and **Colors** menu items:

```
// update the embedded help content panel
viewer.setCurrentID("typefaces");
  ...
// update the embedded help content panel
viewer.setCurrentID("colors");
```

3. Compile (*javac*) and run (*java*) the revised TypeFacer application.

Updating an event handler is really the same as initializing the embedded content viewer: you use the `setCurrentID()` method to specify a map ID. Use this programmatic control of the viewer in event handlers or in response to other actions such as clicking a **Help** button or jumping to a bookmark.

NOTE   This implementation has a potentially undesirable side effect. When
            the user switches to a different screen in the application, the embed-
            ded help topic changes automatically, but the user might still need
            the information in the topic that just disappeared. You can improve
            this behavior by having the application query the content viewer for
            the currently displayed help topic and, based on that answer, decide
            whether or not to switch topics.

This implementation of screen-level embedded help duplicates the screen-level
context-sensitive help you programmed earlier in this chapter. Thus, you might
want to eliminate the **Help → For This Screen** menu item. However, it makes sense
to maintain the interface to the (nonembedded, noncontext-sensitive) HelpSet
Viewer, accessed through the **Help → Contents** menu item. It also makes sense to
continue using the standard HelpSet Viewer to display field-level help. If you want
the field-level help to appear in the embedded help viewer, you must write a custom `HelpBroker` that references your components. This task isn't trivial, but it is
certainly not impossible.

Hiding embedded help

Hiding and displaying components at runtime is not really a JavaHelp topic, but
it's important to embedded help systems. The idea is simple: provide a toggle for
users to specify whether or not they want to see embedded help. If they don't want
embedded help, remove the components. If they do want embedded help, put the
components back.

Use the following steps to implement toggling of the embedded help display. For
this revision of the program, all the lines to be uncommented start with `//#7`.

1. Add an item to the **Help** menu and initialize it as a "hide" toggle:

```
JMenuItem embeddedItem;
   ...
embeddedItem = new JMenuItem("Hide Embedded Help");
helpMenu.add(embeddedItem);
embeddedItem.setActionCommand("hide");
```

2. Activate the menu item, implementing the toggle functionality:

```
// activate the "Embedded Help" toggle menu item

embeddedItem.addActionListener(new ActionListener() {
  public void actionPerformed(ActionEvent ae) {
    if (ae.getActionCommand().equals("hide")) {
      helpPanel.remove(nav);
      helpPanel.remove(viewer);
      helpPanel.validate();
      TypeFacer.this.setSize(500,250);
```

```
        embeddedItem.setText("Show Embedded Help");
        embeddedItem.setActionCommand("show");
    }
    else {
      helpPanel.add(nav);
      helpPanel.add(viewer);
      helpPanel.validate();
      TypeFacer.this.setSize(500,500);
      embeddedItem.setText("Hide Embedded Help");
      embeddedItem.setActionCommand("hide");
    }
  }
});
```

3. Compile (*javac*) and run (*java*) the revised TypeFacer application.

The `ActionListener` first determines whether it needs to hide or show the embedded help panel. It adds or removes the content viewer and navigator components, then resizes the TypeFacer window (so that the layout manager doesn't leave a gaping hole or make the remaining components oddly shaped). Finally, it implements the toggle functionality by changing the wording of the menu item and changing its state with `setActionCommand()`.

The only difference you see in a network version of the previous examples is in the code that finds the HelpSet. For example, if you install your online help on a computer with a web server, you can access the help through a regular URL, as shown in the following code:

```
// Variables to store our HelpSet and HelpBroker:
HelpSet hs;
HelpBroker hb;

// in the constructor, you add this code toward the top
// the assumption here is that the help files exist under the "jh"
// directory that resides in the same directory as the application.
try {
  URL hsURL = new URL("http://your.server.com/jh/HelpSet.hs");
  hs = new HelpSet(null, hsURL);
} catch (Exception ee) {
  System.out.println("HelpSet not found");
  return;
}
hb = hs.createHelpBroker();
```

If you have all your help bundled into a JAR file and wish to run a Java 2 SDK application, use the following JAR URL syntax:

```
URL hsURL = new URL("jar:http://your.server.com/jars/help.jar!/HelpSet.hs");
```

8

Deploying the Help System to Your Users

This chapter discusses issues involved in deploying a JavaHelp-based help system to users—delivering the files in the HelpSet(s) you've developed along with the Java class files that implement the JavaHelp system itself. This chapter covers the following topics:

- Encapsulating the HelpSet
- Delivering all the required files
- Ensuring basic Java support

Encapsulating the HelpSet

A HelpSet can comprise hundreds or even thousands of files. When you deliver your JavaHelp system to users, you probably want to encapsulate each HelpSet into a single Java archive (JAR) file. (Some people call this "JARing the HelpSet.") This is usually preferable for you and your users, avoiding the need to handle vast multitudes of files. It saves space, too: a JAR file is stored in compressed format.

This decision has no effect on the authoring process or on the logical functioning of the JavaHelp system. A HelpSet's directory and file structure work the same way whether encapsulated in a JAR file or stored in the regular filesystem.

Before deciding whether or not to JAR your HelpSet, consider whether users (or you) will need to customize the help topics after they are installed at the user's site. If users need to customize the help topics in your HelpSet, you shouldn't place the HelpSet into a JAR file. Depending on the background of your users, they might not know how to retrieve files from the JAR file or how to JAR the HelpSet files again after they make the updates. If you don't JAR the HelpSet, users can simply use an HTML editor to make changes to individual topic files; the changes are then instantly accessible.

This analysis also applies to you, the HelpSet author. Consider whether you'll be making any updates to the HelpSet after initial installation. Will the HelpSet be merged with other HelpSets or have cross links with them? In such cases, it is most reliable to deliver the entire HelpSet in a single, consistent JAR file.

Creating the JAR File

If you have followed my suggestions for organizing the directory and file structure of your HelpSet, creating a JAR file for the HelpSet should be easy. Use the following steps to create a JAR file for the Aviation HelpSet:

1. At a command prompt, go to the Aviation JavaHelp sample master project directory (*Aviation*).

2. Enter this `jar` command:

```
jar -cvf aviation.jar *
```

   The option flags −cvf specify the options for creating JAR file named *aviation.jar*. The wildcard character * specifies that all files in the current directory (*Aviation*) should be included in the JAR file.

This command creates the JAR file *aviation.jar* in the current directory, *Aviation*. Table 8-1 describes some of the common options you can use with the `jar` command; for creating JAR files, −cvf is typical.

Table 8-1. Option Flags for Creating JAR files

Option Flag	Description
c	Creates a new JAR file
t	Lists the contents of the specified JAR file
x	Extracts the contents of the specified JAR file
f	Signifies that you are specifying the name of the JAR file
v	Lists names of the files placed in, or extracted from, the JAR file

NOTE   Before creating a JAR file for Windows systems, double-check the names of the files and directories specified in your map file (for example, *Map.jhm*). The names in the map file must match the actual file and directory names *exactly*, including upper- and lower-case letters. Windows filesystems look up names in a case-insensitive manner, but JAR files are *case-sensitive* on all platforms. The main indication that you have case problems is when your help topics don't display properly (for example, missing icons or missing content) when you access them through a JAR file, but everything works fine when the HelpSet is accessed from the regular filesystem.

Delivering All the Required Files

This book doesn't discuss particular software installation tools, but here's an informal checklist to help you include all the files required for your help system in your software distribution package. For simplicity, assume that you're deploying a software application and its online documentation, implemented as a single HelpSet.

The application itself

Obviously, you need to include all the files that make up the software application itself.

The HelpSet

If you've encapsulated the HelpSet as a JAR file, just that one file goes into the distribution package. (Exception: if you've excluded the HelpSet file and/or map file from the JAR file, be sure to include those individual files in the distribution package.)

If you're not JARing the HelpSet, you need to include all its files individually.

The Java classes that implement the JavaHelp system

At this time, JavaHelp is an extension to Java, not part of Sun Microsystems' Java software distribution. Thus, you should include the JavaHelp JAR file *jh. jar* or *jhall.jar*, which implements JavaHelp support, in the distribution package. Users must include this JAR file on their Java *class path* when starting a Java application or the HelpSet Viewer, in order to make JavaHelp features available.

A sophisticated installation program might check the user's site, to determine whether the JavaHelp JAR file is already installed. (The user might be installing your software on a computer that already has JavaHelp support, perhaps as part of another one of your company's software distributions.) If so, it may not be necessary to install the JavaHelp JAR file at all.

Alternatively, you can completely separate the installation of the JavaHelp JAR file from the installation of the application and its HelpSet.

Ensuring Basic Java Support

Since JavaHelp itself is implemented in Java, the user's computer must support Java program execution. That is, the computer must have the Java runtime system and class libraries installed. It's beyond the scope of this book to discuss installation of Java itself, but this section discusses some version-related issues.

If you are deploying a Java application and help system based on Java SDK 1.1, you must install support for Java Swing (GUI components) separately. This support is implemented in file *swing.jar*. As with the JavaHelp JAR file, users must include file *swing.jar* on their Java class path. If you are deploying a Java application and help system based on Java 2 (SDK 1.2 and higher), the basic Java distribution includes the Swing classes. Thus, there is no need to provide Swing support separately. Table 8-2 provides more information on version matching.

Table 8-2. Compatible Versions of Java and Java Swing

Java SDK	Java Swing	Notes
1.1	1.1 or 1.1.1	Swing 1.1.1 is included in the JavaHelp distribution. With SDK 1.1, you can't encapsulate HelpSets in JAR files, and you can't print help topics.
1.2	1.1	This version is built into the SDK. To use Swing 1.1.1, upgrade to SDK 1.2.2; overlaying Swing 1.1.1 on SDK 1.2 can be difficult.
1.2.2	1.1.1	This version is built into the SDK.
1.3 (currently at "release candidate" stage)	New version	A new, unnumbered version of Swing is built into the SDK. See *http://java.sun.com/products/jfc/tsc*.

9

Using Third-Party Help-Authoring Tools

Using an HTML document-authoring tool facilitates the creation of HelpSets. Such third-party tools automate many of the JavaHelp development tasks that would otherwise be tedious and time-consuming. To help you make decisions about using third-party authoring tools, this chapter covers the following topics:

- How JavaHelp relates to third-party tools
- How third-party tools work

How JavaHelp Relates to Third-Party Tools

Most third-party help-authoring tools enable you to achieve the cherished goal of "write once, run anywhere." That is, with a single authoring effort, you can create an online help system to be deployed as JavaHelp, WinHelp, or HTML Help.

A good third-party tool attempts to hide the administrative details of JavaHelp. It may even appear that you don't need to understand the workings of the help system, as detailed in the preceding chapters. But a good understanding of JavaHelp aids to diagnose the problems and limitations in the authoring environment. It enables you to go "behind the scenes" to correct or work around such situations. And if you ever need to abandon the third-party tool, you can continue maintaining the help system using the techniques discussed in this book.

How Third-Party Tools Work

Sun Microsystems reports that many help-authoring tools offer or plan to offer JavaHelp support. You should approach the acquisition of a third-party help-authoring tool in the same way you'd purchase any other software:

- Make sure the software offers the features you need and the ease of use you want.

- Make sure the price is right.

- Visit the tool vendors' web sites to get more information on their products. Some offer free trial versions to help you decide if the product is right for you.

Sun's JavaHelp site (*www.java.sun.com/products/javahelp*) lists companies offering JavaHelp third-party tools. Some of the popular products include ForeFront *Fore-Help*, eHelp (formerly Blue Sky) *RoboHELP*, and Wextech *Doc-to-Help*. These products are available for the Windows operating systems; RoboHELP and Doc-to-Help require Microsoft Word. In the remaining sections of this chapter, I discuss how these tools can assist you with help authoring.

ForeHelp

ForeHelp, from ForeFront, is a standalone help-authoring tool. You don't need to use any other application—in particular, Word—in conjunction with it. ForeHelp provides an integrated environment in which you manage projects, write topics, create HelpSet data and navigation files, and enhance the HelpSet.

Creating and setting up a JavaHelp project is fairly easy with ForeHelp. The main flaw, in my opinion, is that ForeHelp doesn't let you organize help topics into a meaningful subdirectory structure as shown in Chapter 3, *Planning the JavaHelp Project*. Instead, ForeHelp places all topic files in one directory. As long as you stay within the ForeHelp authoring environment, this is fine because ForeHelp manages all the data for you. But if you later decide to use the files without ForeHelp, organizing the topics files into subdirectories will be a manual task.

ForeHelp's help-topic editor, shown in Figure 9-1, is similar to Word and other Windows word processors. You can quickly format text, justify paragraphs, and apply HTML tags.

The frame to the left of the topic editor shows all the project's help topics. To edit a particular topic, you simply select it from the list. This opens the topic "file" and loads it into the editor. (Actually, ForeHelp maintains all of a project's topics in a single database. It doesn't create separate HTML-format files until you "build" the project.)

As you create help topics, you don't have to worry about assigning map IDs or help topic filenames because ForeHelp automatically assigns them for you.

You may recall from Chapter 5, *Creating HelpSet Data and Navigation Files*, that creating a JavaHelp TOC file was a detailed manual task. ForeHelp makes this process much easier. The Contents Editor, shown in Figure 9-2, provides a simple and convenient interface for organizing your topics into a hierarchy. (In the

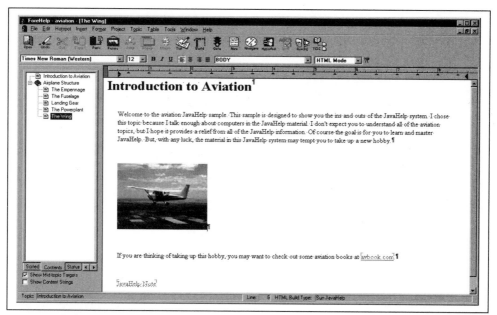

Figure 9-1. ForeHelp's topic editor

ForeHelp model, a category is represented by a book icon; JavaHelp uses a folder icon.) ForeHelp makes it particularly easy to keep track of which topics you've included in the TOC.

ForeHelp also provides a convenient interface for creating a project's index. You use a keyword editor to specify index items for each help topic. When you build the help system, ForeHelp creates an alphabetized index file automatically.

Creating the word-search index is the easiest of all: ForeHelp generates it automatically when you build your JavaHelp project.

In Chapter 6, *Enhancing the HelpSet*, I showed you different ways to enhance your HelpSet. ForeHelp provides features for making these enhancements easy. For example, you can specify that a topic should appear as a pop-up or in a secondary window.

ForeHelp provides a great feature for specifying related topics within each of your help topics. You use a wizard to set up relationships between topics, as shown in Figure 9-3.

When the help system is running, a button or text (depending on which you choose during development) appears in each of the related topics. When the user clicks the button or text, the help system displays a related topics window, as shown in Figure 9-4.

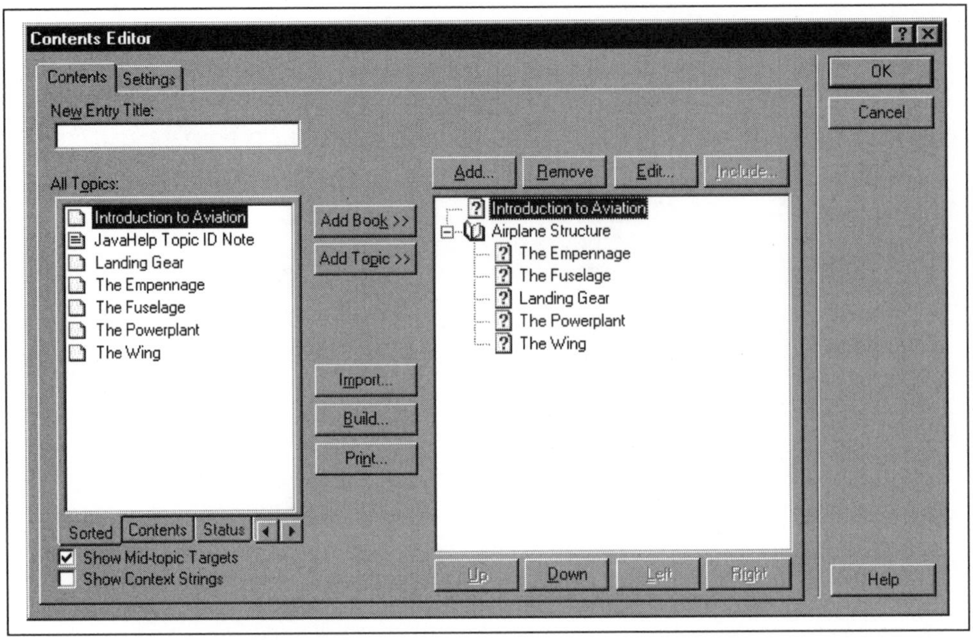

Figure 9-2. ForeHelp's Contents Editor

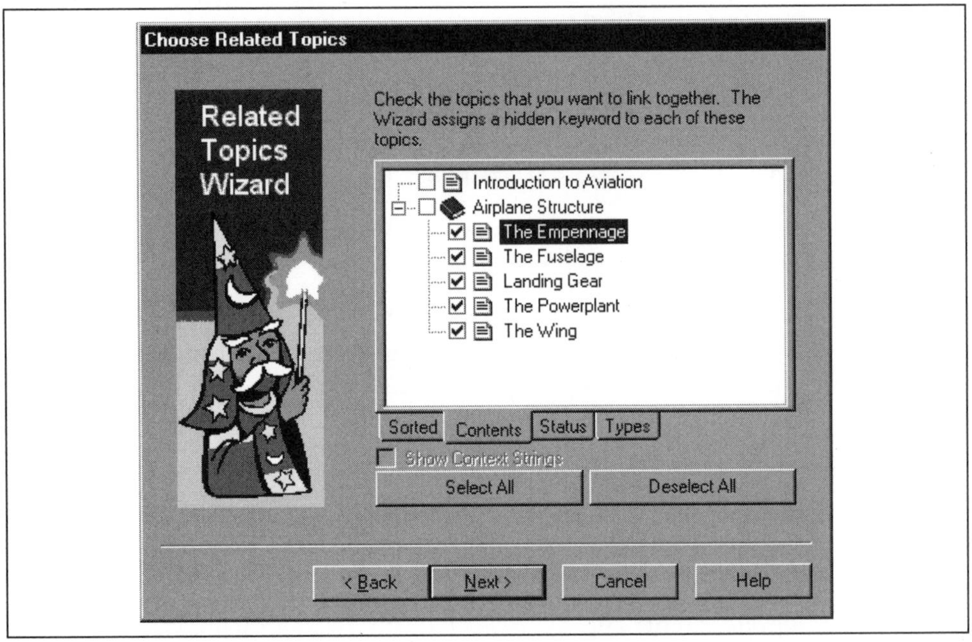

Figure 9-3. ForeHelp's related topics wizard

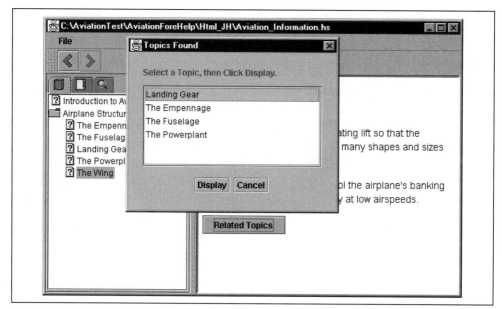

Figure 9-4. ForeHelp's related topics selection dialog

When the user selects a topic from this window, the topic appears in the content pane.

Finally, ForeHelp offers the JavaHelp Settings window, shown in Figure 9-5, for specifying JavaHelp navigation alternatives such as including or excluding navigation components, adding new navigation tabs, and editing existing navigation tabs.

You can also use this window to merge HelpSets and to use and specify a JAR file. If you choose to use a JAR file, ForeHelp automatically compresses and encapsulates the HelpSet files into a JAR when you invoke the compile command.

You can get more information on ForeHelp and download a free preview release of ForeFront software from their web site at *http://www.ff.com.*

Doc-to-Help and RoboHELP

Doc-to-Help and RoboHELP both depend on Word being installed on your computer. This dependency could be a main reason for not using those tools: extra expense. On the other hand, authors who already use Word may adapt to these tools more quickly, given their familiarity with the Word user interface.

The integration with Word offers the ability to create both online help and hardcopy documents from the same source. While this feature enables you to save time by creating two types of documentation at the same time, many professional writers, including myself, argue that online help and hardcopy documents

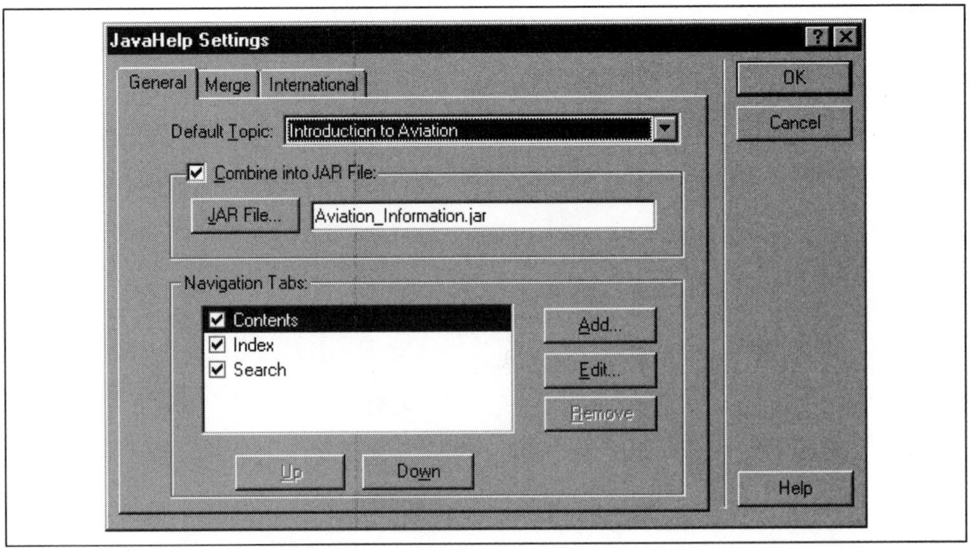

Figure 9-5. ForeHelp's JavaHelp settings window

should be created separately. Because of the way users use online help versus hardcopy documents, you shouldn't use the same format and style for both types of documentation.

Like ForeHelp, the Word-dependent tools provide a friendly graphical interface to assist you with managing projects, writing topics, creating HelpSet data and navigation files, and enhancing a HelpSet. Writing the help topics is somewhat different, since you write the topics in Word itself. The tools offer functions to extend Word's capability so that you can manage your online help project.

Most of the functions in the Word-dependent tools are similar to the functions in ForeHelp; they all use graphical components to make the help development process easy.

You can get more information on these third-party tools from the companies' web sites. At the WexTech web site, *http://www.wextech.com*, you can download a free trial version of Doc-to-Help. A free trial version of RoboHELP is available at eHelp's web site, *http://www.ehelp.com*.

A

HelpSet Tags

A JavaHelp HelpSet contains the following XML-format files:

- Map file

- Table of contents (TOC) file

- Index file

- HelpSet file

These files are discussed in Chapter 5, *Creating HelpSet Data and Navigation Files,* and Chapter 6, *Enhancing the HelpSet.* This appendix provides a quick reference to the XML elements and attributes used in these files.

Map File

Example:

```
<map version="1.0">
  <mapID target="img.toplevelfolder" url="Images/toplevel.gif"/>
  <mapID target="intro" url="Topics/introduction_to_aviation.htm"/>
</map>
```

Tag	Attribute	Required	Description
`<map>`		Yes	Top-level element, encompassing the entire map file. Nested within are elements that define the map IDs for the HelpSet.
	`version`	No	Version of JavaHelp for which the map file is created.
`<mapID>`		Yes	Defines one map ID, associating it with a help topic's URL.

Tag	Attribute	Required	Description
	target	Yes	Map ID, or shorthand name for a help topic. Used throughout JavaHelp to refer to that topic.
	url	Yes	URL of the help topic's HTML file.

TOC File

Example:

```
<toc version="1.0">
  <tocitem image="img.toplevelfolder" target="intro"
           text="Introduction to Aviation">
  <tocitem text="Airplane Structure">
      <tocitem target="empennage" text="Empennage"/>
      <tocitem target="fuselage" text="Fuselage"/>
  </tocitem>
  </toc>
```

Tag	Attribute	Required	Description
`<toc>`		Yes	Top-level element, encompassing the entire TOC file. Nested within are `<tocitem>` elements, which define individual TOC entries.
	version	No	Version of JavaHelp for which the TOC file is created.
`<tocitem>`		Yes	Specifies an individual TOC entry.
	target	No	Map ID of a help topic. If you use this attribute, the TOC entry becomes a link to the specified help topic. Omit this attribute for a TOC entry that is just a heading, not a link.
	text	Yes	Text of the TOC entry, as it appears in the TOC.
	image	No	Map ID of an icon that is displayed along with the text of the TOC entry.

Index File

Example:

```
<index version="1.0">
  <indexitem text="forces">
    <indexitem target="drag" text="drag"/>
    <indexitem target="lift" text="lift"/>
  </indexitem>
  </index>
```

Tag	Attribute	Required	Description
`<index>`		Yes	Top-level element, encompassing the entire index file. Nested within are `<indexitem>` elements, which define individual index entries.
	`version`	No	Version of JavaHelp for which the index file is created.
`<indexitem>`		Yes	Specifies an individual index entry.
	`target`	No	Map ID of a help topic. If you use this attribute, the index entry becomes a link to the specified help topic. You may want to omit this attribute for an index entry that has secondary entries nested within it.
	`text`	Yes	Text of the index entry.

HelpSet File

Example:

```
<?xml version='1.0' encoding='ISO-8859-1' ?>
<!DOCTYPE helpset
   PUBLIC "-//Sun Microsystems Inc.//DTD JavaHelp HelpSet Version 1.0//EN"
          "http://java.sun.com/products/javahelp/helpset_1_0.dtd">

<helpset version="1.0">
  <title>Aviation Information</title>
  <maps>
    <homeID>intro</homeID>
    <mapref location="Map.jhm"/>
  </maps>
  <view>
    <name>TOC</name>
    <label>Aviation TOC</label>
    <type>javax.help.TOCView</type>
    <data>TOC.xml</data>
  </view>
  <view>
    <name>Index</name>
    <label>Aviation Index</label>
    <type>javax.help.IndexView</type>
    <data>Index.xml</data>
  </view>
  <view>
    <name>Search</name>
    <label>Aviation Word Search</label>
    <type>javax.help.SearchView</type>
    <data engine="com.sun.java.help.search.DefaultSearchEngine">
```

```
        JavaHelpSearch
      </data>
    </view>
  </helpset>
```

Tag	Attribute	Required	Description
<helpset>		Yes	Top-level element, encompassing the entire HelpSet file.
	version	No	Version of JavaHelp for which the HelpSet file is created.
<title>		No	Title that appears in the HelpSet Viewer's titlebar. If you omit this element, the titlebar displays Unnamed HelpSet.
<maps>		Yes	Contains subelements (<homeID> and <mapref>) that describe properties related to the HelpSet's map file.
<homeID>		No	Map ID of the default help topic, displayed when the HelpSet Viewer opens the HelpSet. This is a subelement of <maps>.
<mapref>		Yes	Specifies the HelpSet's map file through the location attribute. This is a subelement of <maps>.
	location	Yes	URL of the HelpSet's map file.
<view>		Yes, one for each of the Helpset's navigational components	Defines one navigation component for the HelpSet: TOC, index, or word-search index. Contains subelements <name>, <label>, <type>, and <data>.
<name>		Yes	Specifies the internal Java-level name for the navigation component. This is a subelement of <view>.
<label>		Yes	Specifies the text that appears in the tool tip label when you rest the cursor over the navigation component's tab in the HelpSet Viewer. This is a subelement of <view>.
<type>		Yes	Specifies the Java class to handle the navigation component. For Sun's default navigation components, use: javax.help.TOCView for the TOC, javax.help.IndexView for the index, and javax.help.SearchView for the word-search index. This is a subelement of <view>.

Tag	Attribute	Required	Description
`<data>`		Yes	URL of the file or directory that provides the navigation component's data. Examples: file *Index.xml* for an index component; directory *JavaHelp Search* for a word-search index component. This is a subelement of `<view>`.
	`engine`	Yes, for word-search index only	Specifies the Java class that implements the search engine used for the word-search index. For Sun's default search engine, use `com.sun.java.help.search.DefaultSearchEngine`.
`<subhelpset>`		No	Specifies, through the `location` attribute, another HelpSet to be merged with the current HelpSet.
	`location`	Yes	URL of the HelpSet to be merged with the current HelpSet.

B

Lightweight Component Tags

During JavaHelp development, you can add code to certain help topic (HTML) files to employ the pop-up and secondary window lightweight components.

These components are discussed in Chapter 6, *Enhancing the HelpSet*. This appendix provides you with a quick reference to the elements and attributes that specify the components.

Pop-up and Secondary Windows

Example:

```
<object classid="java:com.sun.java.help.impl.JHSecondaryViewer">
    <param name="viewerActivator" value="javax.help.LinkLabel">
    <param name="viewerStyle" value="javax.help.SecondaryWindow">
    <param name="viewerLocation" value="400,200">
    <param name="viewerSize" value="600,300">
    <param name="text" value="Runway markings">
    <param name="textFontSize" value="medium">
    <param name="textFontWeight" value="plain">
    <param name="id" value="sec.runwaymarkings">
</object>
```

Elements and Attributes

Tag	Attribute	Required	Description
`<object>`		Yes	Element that defines a pop-up or secondary window. Contains one or more `<param>` subelements to specify the window's properties.
	`classid`	Yes	Specifies the Java class that handles the display of the pop-up or secondary window. For Sun's default pop-up and secondary window components, use: `java:com.sun.java.help.impl.JHSecondaryViewer`.
`<param>`		Yes	Specifies, through its `name` and `value` attributes, one property for a pop-up or secondary window. This is a subelement of `<object>`.
	`name`	Yes	Specifies a property to be set. Refer to the next table for the properties' names.
	`value`	Yes	Specifies the value for the property. Refer to the next table for allowable property values.

Parameter Names and Values

Parameter Name	Value	Description
`viewerActivator`		Specifies a Java class, indicating how the pop-up or secondary window is launched.
	`javax.help.LinkLabel`	Launches window with a label (a text string or image). Specifies a text string with the `text` parameter; specifies an image with the `iconByName` or `iconByID` parameter.
	`javax.help.LinkButton`	Launches window with a button, which can have a text string or image. Specifies a text string with the `text` parameter; specifies an image with the `iconByName` or `iconByID` parameter.
`viewerLocation`		Specifies the secondary window's location on the screen. Not used for pop-up windows.
	Any valid pixels setting in `x,y` format	Specifies the position, in pixels, of the secondary window's upper-left corner. `x` =horizontal, `y` =vertical. The upper-left corner of the screen is position `0,0`.
`viewerName`		Specifies a name for the secondary window. Not used for pop-up windows.
	Any window name	Any character string.
`viewerSize`		Specifies the size of the pop-up or secondary window.

Parameter Name	Value	Description
	Any valid pixels setting in x,y format	Window's width (x) and height (y), in pixels.
viewerStyle		Specifies a Java class, indicating the type of window to open (pop-up window or secondary window).
	javax.help. Popup	Pop-up window.
	javax.help. SecondaryWindow	Secondary window.
id		Specifies the help topic to be displayed in the pop-up or secondary window. Alternatively, you can use the content parameter.
	Map ID of a help topic	Any map ID, defined in the HelpSet's map file, that identifies a help-topic file.
content		Specifies the help topic to be displayed in the pop-up or secondary window. Alternatively, you can use the id parameter.
	URL of a help topic	A relative URL (relative to the file containing the current help topic), specifying a help topic file.
iconByID		Specifies an image to be used as the link that launches the pop-up or secondary window. Alternatively, you can use the iconByName or text parameter.
	Map ID of an image	Any map ID, defined in the HelpSet's map file, that identifies an image file.
iconByName		Specifies an image to be used as the link that launches the pop-up or secondary window. This parameter is used only in situations where an image is used for the link. Alternatively, you can use the iconByID or text parameter.
	URL of an image	A relative URL (relative to file containing the current help topic), specifying an image file.
text		Specifies the text string to be used as the link that launches the pop-up or secondary window.
	Any text string	Depending on the viewerActivator setting, this text string appears in the normal text flow or on a button.

Parameter Name	Value	Description
textColor	black blue cyan darkGray gray green lightGray magenta orange pink red white yellow	Specifies the color of any text being used in a link to a pop-up or secondary window.
textFontFamily	Serif SansSerif Monospaced Dialog DialogInput Symbol	Specifies the font family of the string specified as the text value.
textFontSize		Specifies the size of the string specified as the text value.
	xx-small	The smallest font size.
	x-small	
	small	
	medium	
	large	
	x-large	
	xx-large	The largest font size.
	bigger	Increases the size by one level, on the scale between xx-small and xx-large.
	smaller	Decreases the size by one level, on the scale between xx-small and xx-large.
	$n$pt	Sets the font size to n points.
	+n	Increases the current font by n levels, on the scale between xx-small and xx-large.
	-n	Decreases the current font by n levels, on the scale between xx-small and xx-large.
	n	Sets the font size level n (0=xx-small; 6=xx-large).
textFontStyle	plain italic	Specifies the style of the string specified as the text value.
textFontWeight	plain bold	Specifies the weight of the string specified as the text value.

C

The JavaHelp API

This appendix describes the classes in Version 1.1 of the Java programming libraries ("packages") javax.help and javax.help.event.

Classes in Package javax.help

BadIDException

This exception is thrown when creating an ID with invalid arguments or using an ID that does not exist in the specified HelpSet. The getID() method returns the offending ID.

```
public class BadIDException extends IllegalArgumentException {
// Constructors
  public BadIDException(String msg, Map map, String id, HelpSet hs)
// Instance Methods
  public HelpSet getHelpSet()
  public String getID()
  public Map getMap()
}
```

CSH

This Context Sensitive Help (CSH) class provides many static convenience routines that help retrofit existing components with JavaHelp-specific properties. You can also create instances of its three inner classes for simple help-event handling. The CSH.DisplayHelpAfterTracking class, in particular, supports the field-level context sensitive help events.

```
public class CSH {
  // Inner Classes
    public static class DisplayHelpAfterTracking implements ActionListener
    public static class DisplayHelpFromFocus implements ActionListener
    public static class DisplayHelpFromSource implements ActionListener
  // Constructors
    public CSH()
  // Static Methods
    public static String getHelpIDString(Component comp)
    public static String getHelpIDString(MenuItem comp)
    public static HelpSet getHelpSet(Component comp)
    public static HelpSet getHelpSet(MenuItem comp)
    public static void setHelpIDString(Component comp, String helpID)
    public static void setHelpIDString(MenuItem comp, String helpID)
    public static void setHelpSet(Component comp, HelpSet hs)
    public static void setHelpSet(MenuItem comp, HelpSet hs)
    public static Object trackCSEvents()
}
```

DefaultHelpBroker

You typically get a DefaultHelpBroker when you grab the HelpBroker from an
instantiated HelpSet. It is the default implementation of the HelpBroker interface. If you are thinking of building your own broker (to play better with an
embedded help system, for example) the source for this class is a good place to
start.

```
public class DefaultHelpBroker implements HelpBroker, KeyListener {
  // Instance Fields
    protected ActionListener displayHelpFromFocus;
    protected ActionListener displayHelpFromSource;
    protected Font font;
    protected JFrame frame;
    protected HelpSet helpset;
    protected JHelp jhelp;
    protected Locale locale;
    protected JDialog dialog;
    protected Window ownerWindow;
    protected boolean modallyActivated;
  // Constructors
    public DefaultHelpBroker()
    public DefaultHelpBroker(HelpSet hs)
  // Instance Methods
    public void enableHelp(Component comp, String id, HelpSet hs)
    public void enableHelp(MenuItem comp, String id, HelpSet hs)
    public void enableHelpKey(Component comp, String id, HelpSet hs)
    public void enableHelpOnButton(Component comp, String id, HelpSet hs)
    public void enableHelpOnButton(MenuItem comp, String id, HelpSet hs)
    public Map.ID getCurrentID()
```

```
    public URL getCurrentURL()
    public String getCurrentView()
    protected ActionListener getDisplayHelpFromFocus()
    protected ActionListener getDisplayHelpFromSource()
    public Font getFont()
    public HelpSet getHelpSet()
    public Locale getLocale()
    public Point getLocation() throws UnsupportedOperationException
    public Dimension getSize() throws UnsupportedOperationException
    public void initPresentation()
    public boolean isDisplayed()
    public boolean isViewDisplayed()
    public void keyPressed(KeyEvent e)
    public void keyReleased(KeyEvent e)
    public void keyTyped(KeyEvent e)
    public void setActivationWindow(Window window)
    public void setCurrentID(String id) throws BadIDException
    public void setCurrentID(Map.ID id) throws InvalidHelpSetContextException
    public void setCurrentURL(URL url)
    public void setCurrentView(String name)
    public void setDisplayed(boolean b)
    public void setFont(Font f)
    public void setHelpSet(HelpSet hs)
    public void setLocale(Locale l)
    public void setLocation(Point p) throws UnsupportedOperationException
    public void setSize(Dimension d) throws UnsupportedOperationException
    public void setViewDisplayed(boolean displayed)
}
```

DefaultHelpModel

This basic implementation of the HelpModel interface provides the real support
for the text displayed in the help viewer. This implementation handles extra document properties including any highlights shown.

```
public class DefaultHelpModel implements TextHelpModel, Serializable {
  // Inner Classes
    public static class DefaultHighlight implements TextHelpModel.Highlight
  // Instance Fields
    protected PropertyChangeSupport changes;
    protected EventListenerList listenerList;
    protected EventListenerList textListenerList;
  // Constructors
    public DefaultHelpModel(HelpSet hs)
  // Instance Methods
    public void addHelpModelListener(HelpModelListener l)
    public void addHighlight(int pos0, int pos1)
    public void addPropertyChangeListener(PropertyChangeListener l)
    public void addTextHelpModelListener(TextHelpModelListener l)
```

```
        protected void fireHighlightsChanged(Object source)
        protected void fireIDChanged(Object source, Map.ID id, URL url)
        public Map.ID getCurrentID()
        public URL getCurrentURL()
        public String getDocumentTitle()
        public HelpSet getHelpSet()
        public TextHelpModel.Highlight[] getHighlights()
        public void removeAllHighlights()
        public void removeHelpModelListener(HelpModelListener l)
        public void removePropertyChangeListener(PropertyChangeListener l)
        public void removeTextHelpModelListener(TextHelpModelListener l)
        public void setCurrentID(Map.ID ident) throws InvalidHelpSetContextException
        public void setCurrentURL(URL url)
        public void setDocumentTitle(String title)
        public void setHelpSet(HelpSet H)
        public void setHighlights(TextHelpModel.Highlight[] h)
    }
```

FlatMap

A simple implementation of a map intended for one file. You can analyze a file
through this map using the getAllIDs() method.

```
    public class FlatMap implements Map {
    // Constants
        public static final String publicIDString;
    // Constructors
        public FlatMap(URL base, HelpSet hs) throws java.io.IOException
    // Instance Methods
        public Enumeration getAllIDs()
        public Map.ID getClosestID(URL url)
        public HelpSet getHelpSet()
        public Map.ID getIDFromURL(URL url)
        public Enumeration getIDs(URL url)
        public URL getURLFromID(Map.ID iden) throws java.net.MalformedURLException
        public boolean isID(URL url)
        public boolean isValidID(String id, HelpSet hs)
    }
```

HelpBroker

This interface is the basis for all interaction between the programmer and the
help system for an application. The HelpBroker contains a reference to a
HelpSet (which may include sub-HelpSets) and ties your application to that
HelpSet. You can enable and disable help for components with enableHelp().
This interface consists mostly of property accessor/mutator methods, which is
exactly the right way to think of it: this is your interface to the properties of the
help system for this application. For example, using a method such as

setCurrentID(), you can display a particular help topic programmatically at any time. Notice that you are not tied to one HelpSet for the duration of the broker; getHelpSet() and setHelpSet() can find whichever set you are currently viewing, and change it if necessary.

```
public abstract interface HelpBroker {
// Instance Methods
    public abstract void enableHelp(Component comp, String id, HelpSet hs)
    public abstract void enableHelp(MenuItem comp, String id, HelpSet hs)
    public abstract void enableHelpKey(Component comp, String id, HelpSet hs)
    public abstract void enableHelpOnButton(Component comp, String id,
        HelpSet hs) throws java.lang.IllegalArgumentException
    public abstract void enableHelpOnButton(MenuItem comp, String id, HelpSet hs)
    public abstract Map.ID getCurrentID()
    public abstract URL getCurrentURL()
    public abstract String getCurrentView()
    public abstract Font getFont()
    public abstract HelpSet getHelpSet()
    public abstract Locale getLocale()
    public abstract Point getLocation() throws UnsupportedOperationException
    public abstract Dimension getSize() throws UnsupportedOperationException
    public abstract void initPresentation()
    public abstract boolean isDisplayed()
    public abstract boolean isViewDisplayed()
    public abstract void setCurrentID(String id) throws BadIDException
    public abstract void setCurrentID(Map.ID id) throws
        InvalidHelpSetContextException
    public abstract void setCurrentURL(URL url)
    public abstract void setCurrentView(String name)
    public abstract void setDisplayed(boolean displayed) throws
        UnsupportedOperationException
    public abstract void setFont(Font f)
    public abstract void setHelpSet(HelpSet hs)
    public abstract void setLocale(Locale l)
    public abstract void setLocation(Point l) throws UnsupportedOperationException
    public abstract void setSize(Dimension d) throws UnsupportedOperationException
    public abstract void setViewDisplayed(boolean displayed)
}
```

HelpModel

Following the Java Swing GUI component approach, this interface is the model behind a JHelp component. While you can certainly access some of the lower-level properties through this interface, you will most often rely on the HelpBroker to do this work. You can, however, register listeners for model changes with the addHelpModelListener() method. This can be useful for remote monitoring of the topics a user browses.

```
    public abstract interface HelpModel {
     // Instance Methods
       public abstract void addHelpModelListener(HelpModelListener l)
       public abstract void addPropertyChangeListener(PropertyChangeListener l)
       public abstract Map.ID getCurrentID()
       public abstract URL getCurrentURL()
       public abstract HelpSet getHelpSet()
       public abstract void removeHelpModelListener(HelpModelListener l)
       public abstract void removePropertyChangeListener(PropertyChangeListener l)
       public abstract void setCurrentID(Map.ID id) throws
          InvalidHelpSetContextException
       public abstract void setCurrentURL(URL url)
       public abstract void setHelpSet(HelpSet hs)
    }
```

HelpSet

This class is the basis for the entire JavaHelp system. It stores references to the topic files, indexes, TOC entries, etc., for any given help set. The static findHelpSet() method returns a URL to the requested HelpSet that can then create an instance of that HelpSet. From there, use the createHelpBroker() method to get a broker. Once you have the broker in place, you usually work directly with that object.

```
    public class HelpSet {
     // Constants
       public static final String helpBrokerClass;
       public static final String helpBrokerLoader;
       public static final Object implRegistry;
       public static final Object kitLoaderRegistry;
       public static final Object kitTypeRegistry;
       public static final String publicIDString;
     // Instance Fields
       protected EventListenerList listenerList;
     // Constructors
       public HelpSet()
       public HelpSet(ClassLoader loader)
       public HelpSet(ClassLoader loader, URL helpset) throws HelpSetException
     // Static Methods
       public static URL findHelpSet(ClassLoader cl, String name)
       public static URL findHelpSet(ClassLoader cl, String shortName, String
          extension, Locale locale)
       public static URL findHelpSet(ClassLoader cl, String name, Locale locale)
       public static HelpSet parse(URL url, ClassLoader loader, HelpSetFactory
          factory)
     // Instance Methods
       public void add(HelpSet hs)
       public void addHelpSetListener(HelpSetListener l)
```

```
    protected void addSubHelpSet(HelpSet hs)
    protected void addView(NavigatorView view)
    public boolean contains(HelpSet hs)
    public HelpBroker createHelpBroker()
    protected void fireHelpSetAdded(Object source, HelpSet helpset)
    protected void fireHelpSetRemoved(Object source, HelpSet helpset)
    public Map getCombinedMap()
    public URL getHelpSetURL()
    public Enumeration getHelpSets()
    public Map.ID getHomeID()
    public Object getKeyData(Object context, String key)
    public ClassLoader getLoader()
    public Map getLocalMap()
    public Locale getLocale()
    public NavigatorView getNavigatorView(String name)
    public NavigatorView; getNavigatorViews()
    public String getTitle()
    public void parseInto(URL url, HelpSetFactory factory)
    public boolean remove(HelpSet hs)
    public void removeHelpSetListener(HelpSetListener l)
    public void setHomeID(String homeID)
    public void setKeyData(Object context, String key, Object data)
    public void setLocalMap(Map map)
    public void setTitle(String title)
    public String toString()   // Overrides java.lang.Object
}
```

HelpSetException

This exception is thrown from the HelpSet constructor as a generic indication
that something went wrong creating the HelpSet.

```
    public class HelpSetException extends Exception {
    // Constructors
      public HelpSetException(String s)
    }
```

HelpUtilities

These static methods provide a number of convenience methods for handling
such matters as JavaBeans mapping and localized resources.

```
    public class HelpUtilities implements PropertyChangeListener {
    // Constructors
      private HelpUtilities()
    // Static Methods
      public static synchronized Enumeration getCandidates(Locale locale)
      public static String getHelpSetNameFromBean(Class beanClass)
      public static String getIDStringFromBean(Class beanClass)
```

```
        public static ImageIcon getImageIcon(Class baseClass, String image)
        public static Locale getLocale(Component c)
        public static URL getLocalizedResource(ClassLoader cl, String front, String
            back, Locale locale)
        public static URL getLocalizedResource(ClassLoader cl, String front, String
            back, Locale locale, boolean tryRead)
        public static String getString(Locale l, String key)
        public static String getString(String key)
        public static String[] getStringArray(Locale l, String key)
        public static String getText(Locale l, String key)
        public static String getText(Locale l, String key, String s1)
        public static String getText(Locale l, String key, String s1, String s2)
        public static String getText(Locale l, String key, String s1, String s2, String
            s3)
        public static String getText(String key)
        public static String getText(String key, String s1)
        public static String getText(String key, String s1, String s2)
        public static String getText(String key, String s1, String s2, String s3)
        public static boolean isStringInString(java.text.RuleBasedCollator rbc, String
            source, String target)
        public static Locale localeFromLang(String lang)
    // Instance Methods
        public void propertyChange(PropertyChangeEvent event)
    }
```

IndexItem

This class represents individual index items. The HelpSet property for the item
represents the containing set for the Map.ID. Most programmers don't need this
class.

```
    public class IndexItem extends TreeItem {
     // Constructors
        public IndexItem()
        public IndexItem(Map.ID id, Locale locale)
        public IndexItem(Map.ID id, HelpSet hs, Locale locale)
     // Instance Methods
        public HelpSet getHelpSet()
    }
```

IndexView

This class contains support information for an index navigation view (such as
JHelpIndexNavigator). Most programmers don't need this class.

```
    public class IndexView extends NavigatorView {
     // Constants
        public static final String publicIDString;
```

```
   // Inner Classes
     public static class DefaultIndexFactory implements TreeItemFactory
   // Constructors
     public IndexView(HelpSet hs, String name, String label, Hashtable params)
     public IndexView(HelpSet hs, String name, String label, Locale locale,
        Hashtable params)
   // Static Methods
     public static DefaultMutableTreeNode parse(URL url, HelpSet hs,
        Locale locale, TreeItemFactory factory)
   // Instance Methods
     // Overrides NavigatorView
     public abstract Component createNavigator(HelpModel model)
     public DefaultMutableTreeNode getDataAsTree()
}
```

InvalidHelpSetContextException

This exception is thrown when setting the current ID on a sub-HelpSet that is not valid for the current help model.

```
   public class InvalidHelpSetContextException extends Exception {
   // Constructors
     public InvalidHelpSetContextException(String msg, HelpSet context, HelpSet hs)
   // Instance Methods
     public HelpSet getContext()
     public HelpSet getHelpSet()
}
```

InvalidNavigatorViewException

This exception is thrown when a navigator cannot be built from the given parameters to the view constructor. The possible offending parameters can be retrieved from the exception using the various get...() methods.

```
   public class InvalidNavigatorViewException extends Exception {
   // Constructors
     public InvalidNavigatorViewException(String msg, HelpSet hs, String name,
        String label, Locale locale, String className, Hashtable params)
   // Instance Methods
     public String getClassName()
     public HelpSet getHelpSet()
     public String getLabel()
     public Locale getLocale()
     public String getName()
     public Hashtable getParams()
}
```

JHelp

JHelp is a Swing component that contains the navigation and content viewers for a HelpSet. Unless you have specifically built your own viewer or embedded help environment, when users ask for help on a topic, they will view that topic in a JHelp object. You can create one directly from a HelpSet using a public constructor, and then customize it with extra navigators using the addHelpNavigator() method. However, most programmers work with the default navigators; you probably do not need to touch this class at all.

```
public class JHelp extends JComponent implements HelpSetListener, Accessible {
  // Instance Fields
    protected JHelpContentViewer contentViewer;
    protected TextHelpModel helpModel;
    protected boolean navDisplayed;
    protected Vector navigators;
  // Constructors
    public JHelp()
    public JHelp(HelpSet hs)
    public JHelp(TextHelpModel model)
  // Instance Methods
    public void addHelpNavigator(JHelpNavigator navigator)
    public JHelpContentViewer getContentViewer()
    public JHelpNavigator getCurrentNavigator()
    public Enumeration getHelpNavigators()
    public URL getHelpSetURL()
    public TextHelpModel getModel()
    public HelpUI getUI()
    public String getUIClassID()   // Overrides javax.swing.JComponent
    public void helpSetAdded(HelpSetEvent e)
    public void helpSetRemoved(HelpSetEvent e)
    public boolean isNavigatorDisplayed()
    public void removeHelpNavigator(JHelpNavigator navigator)
    public void setCurrentID(Map.ID id) throws InvalidHelpSetContextException
    public void setCurrentID(String id) throws BadIDException
    public void setCurrentNavigator(JHelpNavigator navigator)
    public void setCurrentURL(URL url)
    public void setHelpSetSpec(String spec)
    public void setModel(TextHelpModel newModel)
    public void setNavigatorDisplayed(boolean displayed)
    public void setUI(HelpUI ui)
    protected void setupNavigators()
    public void updateUI()   // Overrides javax.swing.JComponent
}
```

JHelpContentViewer

This class is an implementation of a content viewer for a `HelpSet`. The content viewer shows you the actual contents of a topic as opposed to the navigation viewers that simply allow you to maneuver through a HelpSet. If you create your own JHelpContentViewer object, you can use it to build an embedded help system or a custom help browser with your own navigators. The setCurrentID() and setCurrentURL() methods can be used to switch the currently displayed topic.

```
public class JHelpContentViewer extends JComponent implements Accessible {
  // Instance Fields
    protected TextHelpModel model;
  // Constructors
    public JHelpContentViewer()
    public JHelpContentViewer(HelpSet hs)
    public JHelpContentViewer(TextHelpModel model)
  // Instance Methods
    public void addHelpModelListener(HelpModelListener l)
    public void addHighlight(int p0, int p1)
    public void addTextHelpModelListener(TextHelpModelListener l)
    public EditorKit createEditorKitForContentType(String type)
    public URL getCurrentURL()
    public String getDocumentTitle()
    public TextHelpModel getModel()
    public HelpContentViewerUI getUI()
    public String getUIClassID()   // Overrides javax.swing.JComponent
    public void removeAllHighlights()
    public void removeHelpModelListener(HelpModelListener l)
    public void removeHelpModelListener(TextHelpModelListener l)
    public void setCurrentID(Map.ID id) throws InvalidHelpSetContextException
    public void setCurrentID(String id) throws BadIDException
    public void setCurrentURL(URL url)
    public void setModel(TextHelpModel newModel)
    public void setUI(HelpContentViewerUI ui)
    public void updateUI()   // Overrides javax.swing.JComponent
  }
```

JHelpIndexNavigator

One of the built-in navigators extending JHelpNavigator, this subclass allows you to display and traverse an index of topics.

```
public class JHelpIndexNavigator extends JHelpNavigator {
  // Constructors
    public JHelpIndexNavigator(HelpSet hs, String name, String label, URL data)
       throws InvalidNavigatorViewException
    public JHelpIndexNavigator(NavigatorView view)
    public JHelpIndexNavigator(NavigatorView view, HelpModel model)
```

```
    // Instance Methods
      // Overrides javax.help.JHelpNavigator
      public boolean canMerge(NavigatorView view)
      public String getUIClassID()   // Overrides javax.swing.JComponent
      public void merge(NavigatorView view)   // Overrides javax.help.JHelpNavigator
      public void remove(NavigatorView view) // Overrides javax.help.JHelpNavigator
    }
```

JHelpNavigator

This is the base class for all JHelp navigators. A navigator provides a mechanism
for traversing the topics available in a HelpSet. (The contents of the topics are
shown in the content viewer.) Most of the methods are used in determining the
display information for the navigator—its name, its icon, etc. Beyond that straight-
forward functionality, the merge methods add the most interesting features to this
class. You can test to see if you can merge the information in this navigator with
another, using the canMerge() method. If the navigators can be merged, the
merge() method will accomplish that task.

```
    public class JHelpNavigator extends JComponent implements Accessible {
     // Instance Fields
       protected HelpModel helpModel;
       protected String type;
     // Constructors
       public JHelpNavigator(NavigatorView view)
       public JHelpNavigator(NavigatorView view, HelpModel model)
     // Static Methods
       protected static Hashtable createParams(URL data)
     // Instance Methods
       public void addHelpModelListener(HelpModelListener l)
       public boolean canMerge(NavigatorView view)
       public Icon getIcon()
       public HelpModel getModel()
       public String getNavigatorLabel()
       public String getNavigatorLabel(Locale locale)
       public String getNavigatorName()
       public NavigatorView getNavigatorView()
       public HelpNavigatorUI getUI()
       public String getUIClassID()   // Overrides javax.swing.JComponent
       public void merge(NavigatorView view)
       public void remove(NavigatorView view)
       public void removeHelpModelListener(HelpModelListener l)
       public void setModel(HelpModel newModel)
       public void setUI(HelpNavigatorUI ui)
       public void updateUI()   // Overrides javax.swing.JComponent
    }
```

JHelpSearchNavigator

Another of the built-in navigators (along with JHelpIndexNavigator and
JHelpTOCNavigator) the search navigator allows a user to type in a keyword and
search for an occurrence of that word in the HelpSet. Note that you can specify
your own SearchEngine if you like.

```
public class JHelpSearchNavigator extends JHelpNavigator {
  // Constructors
    public JHelpSearchNavigator(HelpSet hs, String name, String label, URL data)
  throws InvalidNavigatorViewException
    public JHelpSearchNavigator(NavigatorView view)
    public JHelpSearchNavigator(NavigatorView view, HelpModel model)
  // Instance Methods
    public boolean canMerge(NavigatorView view)   // Overrides JHelpNavigator
    protected String getDefaultQueryEngine()
    public SearchEngine getSearchEngine()
    public String getUIClassID()   // Overrides javax.swing.JComponent
    public void merge(NavigatorView view)   // Overrides JHelpNavigator
    public void remove(NavigatorView view)   // Overrides JHelpNavigator
    public void setSearchEngine(SearchEngine search)
}
```

JHelpTOCNavigator

Another of the built-in navigators (along with JHelpIndexNavigator and
JHelpSearchNavigator) this navigator presents a tree-based TOC of the topics
in the HelpSet. The topics are built from the HelpSet dynamically.

```
public class JHelpTOCNavigator extends JHelpNavigator {
  // Constructors
    public JHelpTOCNavigator(HelpSet hs, String name, String label, URL data)
      throws InvalidNavigatorViewException
    public JHelpTOCNavigator(NavigatorView view)
    public JHelpTOCNavigator(NavigatorView view, HelpModel model)
  // Instance Methods
    public boolean canMerge(NavigatorView view)   // Overrides JHelpNavigator
    public String getUIClassID()   // Overrides javax.swing.JComponent
    public void merge(NavigatorView view)   // Overrides JHelpNavigator
    public void remove(NavigatorView view)   // Overrides JHelpNavigator
}
```

Map

This interface defines the relationship between an ID and a URL. The FlatMap
and TryMap classes are example implementations of this interface. You can use the
getAllIDs() method to retrieve a list of the IDs in the map or getIDs() to get a
list of the IDs related to a particular URL. The ID inner class consists solely of two

public fields: id (a `String`) and hs (a `HelpSet`). You can build your own using the `ID.create()` method.

```
public abstract interface Map {
  // Inner Classes
    public static final class ID
  // Instance Methods
    public abstract Enumeration getAllIDs()
    public abstract Map.ID getClosestID(URL url)
    public abstract Map.ID getIDFromURL(URL url)
    public abstract Enumeration getIDs(URL url)
    public abstract URL getURLFromID(Map.ID id)
        throws java.net MalformedURLException
    public abstract boolean isID(URL url)
    public abstract boolean isValidID(String id, HelpSet hs)
}
```

NavigatorView

This class is the collection point for navigator information. The static `create()` method can build a new navigator from scratch. The `createNavigator()` method creates an instance of the navigator tied to the given `HelpModel`.

```
public abstract class NavigatorView {
  // Constructors
    protected NavigatorView(HelpSet hs, String name, String label, Locale locale,
      Hashtable params)
  // Static Methods
    public static NavigatorView create(HelpSet hs, String name, String label,
      Locale locale, String className, Hashtable params)
      throws InvalidNavigatorViewException
  // Instance Methods
    public abstract Component createNavigator(HelpModel model)
    public HelpSet getHelpSet()
    public String getLabel()
    public String getLabel(Locale locale)
    public Locale getLocale()
    public String getName()
    public Hashtable getParameters()
}
```

SearchHit

This class stores information about the position and "confidence" of a search hit.

```
public class SearchHit {
  // Constructors
    public SearchHit(double confidence, int begin, int end)
```

```
  // Instance Methods
    public int getBegin()
    public double getConfidence()
    public int getEnd()
}
```

SearchTOCItem

This extension of the TOCItem class also includes a list of search hits (and related
information) associated with this item.

```
public class SearchTOCItem extends TOCItem {
  // Constructors
    public SearchTOCItem(Map.ID id, Map.ID imageID, HelpSet hs, Locale locale)
    public SearchTOCItem(SearchItem item)
  // Instance Methods
    public void addSearchHit(SearchHit si)
    public double getConfidence()
    public Enumeration getConfidences()
    public Enumeration getSearchHits()
    public URL getURL()
    public int hitCount()
    public boolean inTOC()
}
```

SearchView

This class contains support information for a search navigation view (such as
JHelpSearchNavigator). Most programmers don't need this class.

```
public class SearchView extends NavigatorView {
  // Constructors
    public SearchView(HelpSet hs, String name, String label, Hashtable params)
    public SearchView(HelpSet hs, String name, String label, Locale locale,
      Hashtable params)
  // Instance Methods
    public abstract Component createNavigator(HelpModel model)
      // Overrides javax.help.NavigatorView
}
```

TextHelpModel

This extension of the HelpModel interface adds support for additional text opera-
tions such as the document title and text highlights.

```
public abstract interface TextHelpModel extends HelpModel {
  // Inner Classes
    public abstract static interface Highlight
  // Instance Methods
    public abstract void addHighlight(int pos0, int pos1)
```

```
    public abstract void addTextHelpModelListener(TextHelpModelListener l)
    public abstract String getDocumentTitle()
    public abstract TextHelpModel.Highlight[] getHighlights()
    public abstract void removeAllHighlights()
    public abstract void removeTextHelpModelListener(TextHelpModelListener l)
    public abstract void setDocumentTitle(String title)
    public abstract void setHighlights(TextHelpModel.Highlight[] h)
}
```

TOCItem

This class stores information for a TOC entry, including an optional image (referenced through its own imageID).

```
public class TOCItem extends TreeItem {
  // Constructors
    public TOCItem()
    public TOCItem(Map.ID id, Map.ID imageID, HelpSet hs, Locale locale)
    public TOCItem(Map.ID id, Map.ID imageID, Locale locale)
  // Instance Methods
    public HelpSet getHelpSet()
    public Map.ID getImageID()
}
```

TOCView

This class contains support information for a TOC navigation view (such as JHelpTOCNavigator). The getDataAsTree() method returns a Default-MutableTreeNode (from the javax.swing.tree package) that can be used to build a custom JTree.

```
public class TOCView extends NavigatorView {
  // Constants
    public static final String publicIDString;
  // Inner Classes
    public static class DefaultTOCFactory implements TreeItemFactory
  // Constructors
    public TOCView(HelpSet hs, String name, String label, Hashtable params)
    public TOCView(HelpSet hs, String name, String label, Locale locale, Hashtable
      params)
  // Static Methods
    public static DefaultMutableTreeNode parse(URL url, HelpSet hs, Locale locale,
      TreeItemFactory factory)
  // Instance Methods
    // Overrides javax.help.NavigatorView
    public abstract Component createNavigator(HelpModel model)
    public DefaultMutableTreeNode getDataAsTree()
}
```

TreeItem

This class is the basis for all items displayed in both TOC and Index navigators. You can retrieve an ID object for the item with getID() or a printable name for the item with getName().

```
public class TreeItem {
  // Constructors
    public TreeItem(Map.ID id, Locale locale)
  // Instance Methods
    public Map.ID getID()
    public Locale getLocale()
    public String getName()
    public void setName(String name)
    public String toString()   // Overrides java.lang.Object
}
```

TreeItemFactory

This interface allows you to create and reuse tree building parsers. Most programmers don't need to implement this interface.

```
public abstract interface TreeItemFactory {
  // Instance Methods
    public abstract TreeItem createItem()
    public abstract TreeItem createItem(String tagName, Hashtable attributes,
      HelpSet hs, Locale locale)
    public abstract Enumeration listMessages()
    public abstract DefaultMutableTreeNode parsingEnded(javax.swing.tree.
      DefaultMutableTreeNode node)
    public abstract void parsingStarted(URL source)
    public abstract void processDOCTYPE(String root, String publicID, String
      systemID)
    public abstract void processPI(HelpSet hs, String target, String data)
    public abstract void reportMessage(String msg, boolean validParse)
}
```

TryMap

This class creates an efficient group of Maps that can be used en masse for looking up IDs or checking the validity of a given ID in one of the maps contained in this parent map. You can start quite easily by creating an empty Map with the constructor and then using the add() method to attach other maps.

```
public class TryMap implements Map {
  // Constructors
    public TryMap()
  // Instance Methods
    public void add(Map map)
```

```
      public Enumeration getAllIDs()
      public Map.ID getClosestID(URL url)
      public Map.ID getIDFromURL(URL url)
      public Enumeration getIDs(URL url)
      public Enumeration getMaps()
      public URL getURLFromID(Map.ID id) throws java.net.MalformedURLException
      public boolean isID(URL url)
      public boolean isValidID(String id, HelpSet hs)
      public boolean remove(Map map)
    }
```

UnsupportedOperationException

This exception indicates that a valid API call is not actually supported by the underlying implementation.

```
    public class UnsupportedOperationException extends RuntimeException {
     // Constructors
       public UnsupportedOperationException()
       public UnsupportedOperationException(String message)
    }
```

Classes in Package javax.help.event

EventListenerList

This class is similar in effect and purpose to the EventListenerList found in the Swing package. It serves as a type-safe means of storing several listeners in a single list. You can attach a listener to this list using the add() method. Notice that you specify the class type of the listener in addition to the listener itself. This class type can be used later to filter out a subset of listeners that fit a particular description.

```
    public class EventListenerList implements Serializable {
     // Instance Fields
       protected transient Object[] listenerList;
     // Constructors
       public EventListenerList()
     // Instance Methods
       public synchronized void add(Class t, EventListener l)
       public int getListenerCount(Class t)
       public int getListenerCount()
       public Object; getListenerList()
       public synchronized void remove(Class t, EventListener l)
       public String toString()  // Overrides java.lang.Object
    }
```

HelpModelEvent

This event describes a change in the current `HelpModel`. This could be a change in a specific ID or a change in the highlighting (represented by *pos0* and *pos1*).

```
public class HelpModelEvent extends EventObject {
  // Constructors
    public HelpModelEvent(Object source, int pos0, int pos1)
    public HelpModelEvent(Object source, Map.ID id, URL url)
  // Instance Methods
    public Map.ID getID()
    public int getPos0()
    public int getPos1()
    public URL getURL()
}
```

HelpModelListener

This listener receives notification when the current ID in a `HelpModel` changes. The highlights are automatically reset, but new highlights may be reported through the `HelpModelEvent` passed to the `idChanged()` method.

```
public abstract interface HelpModelListener extends EventListener {
  // Instance Methods
    public abstract void idChanged(HelpModelEvent e)
}
```

HelpSetEvent

This event indicates that a nested `HelpSet` has been added or removed. The `getAction()` method can determine whether the set was added or removed. (It should return one of the constants HELPSET_ADDED or HELPSET_REMOVED.)

```
public class HelpSetEvent extends EventObject {
  // Constants
    public static final int HELPSET_ADDED;
    public static final int HELPSET_REMOVED;
  // Constructors
    public HelpSetEvent(Object source, HelpSet helpset, int action)
  // Instance Methods
    public int getAction()
    public HelpSet getHelpSet()
    public String toString()  // Overrides java.lang.Object
}
```

HelpSetListener

This listener receives notification when a nested `HelpSet` is added or removed.

```
public abstract interface HelpSetListener extends EventListener {
 // Instance Methods
    public abstract void helpSetAdded(HelpSetEvent e)
    public abstract void helpSetRemoved(HelpSetEvent e)
 }
```

TextHelpModelEvent

This event indicates that a change in the `TextHelpModel` has occurred. No model specific information is conveyed through this event; the programmer should query the source for its current state.

```
public class TextHelpModelEvent extends EventObject {
 // Constructors
    public TextHelpModelEvent(Object source)
 }
```

TextHelpModelListener

This listener receives notification when a change to the `TextHelpModel` occurs.

```
public abstract interface TextHelpModelListener extends EventListener {
 // Instance Methods
    public abstract void highlightsChanged(TextHelpModelEvent e)
 }
```

D

TypeFacer.java Source Listing

This appendix contains a listing of the source file, *TypeFacer.java,* for the Typeface Tester application described in Chapter 7, *Using the JavaHelp API for Advanced Presentation Options.* JavaHelp-related code appears in **bold**.

```java
/*
 * TypeFacer.java
 * A simple application for styling sample text.
 *
 * This application serves as the basis for JavaHelp demonstrations:
 * screen-level help, field-level help, and embedded help
 */

// .................................... imports
import java.awt.event.*;
import java.awt.*;
import java.util.Hashtable;
import java.io.*;
import java.net.*;
import javax.swing.*;
import javax.swing.border.*;
import javax.help.*;


// .................................... TypeFacer (frame)

public class TypeFacer extends JFrame {

    // JavaHelp items

    HelpSet hs;
    HelpBroker hb;

    // screen components
```

```
JTextField inputField, displayField;
JComboBox  fontChoice, foreChoice, backChoice;
JCheckBox  boldBox, italicBox;
JButton    showButton, clearButton;
JButton    helpButton;
JButton    qButton;

// embedded help components
JPanel helpPanel;
JHelpNavigator nav;
JHelpContentViewer viewer;

// menu components

JMenu     fileMenu, viewMenu;
JMenuItem exitItem, typeItem, colorItem;
JMenu helpMenu;
JMenuItem helpItem;
JMenuItem helpItemTOC;
JMenuItem embeddedItem;

// frame will contain a panel using the CardLayout manager

CardLayout manager;
JPanel cards;

// fonts and colors for use in display box

Hashtable fonts, colors;

// combo box choices

final String[] fontList =
        { "TimesRoman", "Helvetica", "Courier" };
final String[] colorList =
        { "Black", "Red", "Green", "Yellow", "Blue", "White" };

// title for each screen

final String typefTitle = "Typeface Tester: Choose Typeface";
final String colorTitle = "Typeface Tester: Choose Colors";

// ...................................... constructor

public TypeFacer() {

  // create and size a JFrame; set up content pane
  super("Typeface Tester: Choose Typeface");
```

```
//!!in next line, change "250" to "500"
setSize(500, 250);

JPanel contentPane = (JPanel) getContentPane();
contentPane.setLayout(new FlowLayout());
contentPane.setBorder(
  BorderFactory.createEmptyBorder(10,10,10,10));

// exit the program if the user closes the window

addWindowListener(new WindowAdapter() {
  public void windowClosing(WindowEvent we) {System.exit(0);}
});

// open HelpSet, send console message
// hardcoded location: "HelpSet.hs" in "TFhelp" subdirectory

try {
  URL hsURL = new URL((new File(".")).toURL(), "TFhelp/HelpSet.hs");
  hs = new HelpSet(null, hsURL);
  System.out.println("Found help set at " + hsURL);
}
catch (Exception ee) {
  System.out.println("HelpSet not found");
  System.exit(0);
}

// create HelpBroker from HelpSet
hb = hs.createHelpBroker();
// enable function key F1
hb.enableHelpKey(getRootPane(), "overview", hs);

// set up top-most panel containing text-input field

JPanel inputPanel = new JPanel(new FlowLayout());
contentPane.add(inputPanel);

JLabel inputLabel = new JLabel("Text");
inputField = new JTextField("Enter some text here", 30);

inputPanel.add(inputLabel);
inputPanel.add(inputField);

// set up middle panel, in which two cards will
// be displayed: typefCard and colorCard

manager = new CardLayout();
cards = new JPanel(manager);
contentPane.add(cards);
```

```
JPanel typefCard = new JPanel(new GridLayout(2,4,5,5));
JPanel colorCard = new JPanel(new GridLayout(2,4,5,5));

cards.add(typefCard, "Typefaces");
cards.add(colorCard, "Colors");

// TypeFace card: create components

JLabel fontLabel = new JLabel("Font", JLabel.RIGHT);
fontChoice = new JComboBox(fontList);

JLabel styleLabel = new JLabel("Style", JLabel.RIGHT);
boldBox = new JCheckBox("Bold");
italicBox = new JCheckBox("Italic");

// TypeFace card: place components on card

// first row
typefCard.add(fontLabel);
typefCard.add(fontChoice);
typefCard.add(styleLabel);
typefCard.add(boldBox);
// second row (start with three empty slots)
typefCard.add(new JLabel());
typefCard.add(new JLabel());
typefCard.add(new JLabel());
typefCard.add(italicBox);

// Colors card: create components

JLabel foreLabel = new JLabel("Foreground", JLabel.RIGHT);
foreChoice = new JComboBox(colorList);
foreChoice.setSelectedIndex(0);  // initialize to "black"

JLabel backLabel = new JLabel("Background", JLabel.RIGHT);
backChoice = new JComboBox(colorList);
backChoice.setSelectedIndex(5);  // initialize to "white"

// Colors card: place components on card

// first row
colorCard.add(new JLabel());
colorCard.add(foreLabel);
colorCard.add(foreChoice);
colorCard.add(new JLabel());
// second row
colorCard.add(new JLabel());
colorCard.add(backLabel);
```

```java
colorCard.add(backChoice);
colorCard.add(new JLabel());

// set up styled output panel

JPanel displayPanel = new JPanel(new FlowLayout());
contentPane.add(displayPanel);

displayField = new JTextField(40);
displayField.setEditable(false);
displayField.setFont(new Font("TimesRoman", Font.PLAIN, 16));
displayField.setHorizontalAlignment(SwingConstants.CENTER);

// set up button panel

JPanel buttonPanel =
  new JPanel(new FlowLayout(FlowLayout.CENTER, 5, 5));
contentPane.add(buttonPanel);

showButton = new JButton("Show");
clearButton = new JButton("Clear");
helpButton = new JButton("Help");
qButton = new JButton(new ImageIcon("help.gif"));  // make this an Icon

buttonPanel.add(showButton);
buttonPanel.add(clearButton);
buttonPanel.add(helpButton);
buttonPanel.add(qButton);
displayPanel.add(displayField);

// create an embedded help panel
helpPanel = new JPanel(new GridLayout(1,2,5,5));

// add a content viewer
viewer = new JHelpContentViewer(hs);
viewer.setPreferredSize(new Dimension(200,220));
viewer.setCurrentID("typefaces");

// add a navigator with a table of contents view
nav = (JHelpNavigator)
  hs.getNavigatorView("TOC").createNavigator(viewer.getModel());
nav.setPreferredSize(new Dimension(200,220));

// add the components to the layout
helpPanel.add(nav);
helpPanel.add(viewer);
contentPane.add(helpPanel);

// set up menu structure
```

```java
fileMenu = new JMenu("File");
exitItem = new JMenuItem("Exit");
fileMenu.add(exitItem);

viewMenu = new JMenu("View");
typeItem = new JMenuItem("Typefaces");
colorItem = new JMenuItem("Colors");
viewMenu.add(typeItem);
viewMenu.add(colorItem);

helpMenu = new JMenu("Help");
helpItemTOC = new JMenuItem("Contents");
helpMenu.add(helpItemTOC);
CSH.setHelpIDString(helpItemTOC, "overview");
//!!in next line, change "Contents" to "For This Screen"
helpItem = new JMenuItem("Contents...");
helpMenu.add(helpItem);

embeddedItem = new JMenuItem("Hide Embedded Help");
helpMenu.add(embeddedItem);
embeddedItem.setActionCommand("hide");

JMenuBar menuBar = new JMenuBar();
menuBar.add(fileMenu);
menuBar.add(viewMenu);
menuBar.add(helpMenu);

setJMenuBar(menuBar);

// Fill the fonts and colors hashtables

fonts   = new Hashtable(12);
fonts.put("Helvetica",
        new Font("Helvetica", Font.PLAIN, 16));
fonts.put("Helveticabold",
        new Font("Helvetica", Font.BOLD, 16));
fonts.put("Helveticaitalic",
        new Font("Helvetica", Font.ITALIC, 16));
fonts.put("Helveticabolditalic",
        new Font("Helvetica", Font.BOLD + Font.ITALIC, 16));
fonts.put("TimesRoman",
        new Font("TimesRoman", Font.PLAIN, 16));
fonts.put("TimesRomanbold",
        new Font("TimesRoman", Font.BOLD, 16));
fonts.put("TimesRomanitalic",
        new Font("TimesRoman", Font.ITALIC, 16));
fonts.put("TimesRomanbolditalic",
        new Font("TimesRoman", Font.BOLD + Font.ITALIC, 16));
```

```java
fonts.put("Courier",
        new Font("Courier", Font.PLAIN, 16));
fonts.put("Courierbold",
        new Font("Courier", Font.BOLD, 16));
fonts.put("Courieritalic",
        new Font("Courier", Font.ITALIC, 16));
fonts.put("Courierbolditalic",
        new Font("Courier", Font.BOLD + Font.ITALIC, 16));

colors = new Hashtable(6);
colors.put("Black", Color.black);
colors.put("Red", Color.red);
colors.put("Blue", Color.blue);
colors.put("Green", Color.green);
colors.put("Yellow", Color.yellow);
colors.put("White", Color.white);

// activate the "Show" button

showButton.addActionListener(new ActionListener() {
  public void actionPerformed(ActionEvent ae) {

    // compute the font's name (hash key)
    String fontFace = fontChoice.getSelectedItem().toString();
    fontFace += boldBox.isSelected() ? "bold" : "";
    fontFace += italicBox.isSelected() ? "italic" : "";

    // set the font
    displayField.setFont((Font)fonts.get(fontFace));

    // set the colors
    displayField.setForeground(
      (Color) colors.get(foreChoice.getSelectedItem()));
    displayField.setBackground(
      (Color) colors.get(backChoice.getSelectedItem()));
    displayField.setText(inputField.getText());
  }
});

// activate the "Clear" button

clearButton.addActionListener(new ActionListener() {
  public void actionPerformed(ActionEvent ae) {
    displayField.setText("");
    inputField.setText("");
  }
});

// activate the "Exit" menu item
```

```
exitItem.addActionListener(new ActionListener() {
  public void actionPerformed(ActionEvent ae) {System.exit(0);}
});

// activate the "Typefaces" menu item

typeItem.addActionListener(new ActionListener() {
  public void actionPerformed(ActionEvent ae) {
    manager.show(cards, "Typefaces");
    TypeFacer.this.setTitle(typefTitle);
    // configure function key F1, help button, help menu item
    CSH.setHelpIDString(TypeFacer.this.getRootPane(), "typefaces");
    CSH.setHelpIDString(helpItem, "typefaces");
    CSH.setHelpIDString(helpButton, "typefaces");

    // update the embedded help content panel
    viewer.setCurrentID("typefaces");
  }
});

// activate the "Colors" menu item

colorItem.addActionListener(new ActionListener() {
  public void actionPerformed(ActionEvent ae) {
    manager.show(cards, "Colors");
    TypeFacer.this.setTitle(colorTitle);
    // configure function key F1, help button, help menu item
    CSH.setHelpIDString(TypeFacer.this.getRootPane(), "colors");
    CSH.setHelpIDString(helpItem, "colors");
    CSH.setHelpIDString(helpButton, "colors");

    // update the embedded help content panel
    viewer.setCurrentID("colors");
  }
});

// activate the "Embedded Help" toggle menu item
embeddedItem.addActionListener(new ActionListener() {
  public void actionPerformed(ActionEvent ae) {
    if (ae.getActionCommand().equals("hide")) {
      helpPanel.remove(nav);
      helpPanel.remove(viewer);
      helpPanel.validate();
      TypeFacer.this.setSize(500,250);
      embeddedItem.setText("Show Embedded Help");
      embeddedItem.setActionCommand("show");
    }
    else {
```

```
            helpPanel.add(nav);
            helpPanel.add(viewer);
            helpPanel.validate();
            TypeFacer.this.setSize(500,500);
            embeddedItem.setText("Hide Embedded Help");
            embeddedItem.setActionCommand("hide");
          }
        }
      });


      // activate the field-level help button
      qButton.addActionListener(
        new CSH.DisplayHelpAfterTracking(hb)
      );

      // activate the Help menu item and Help button
      ActionListener helper = new CSH.DisplayHelpFromSource(hb);
      helpItem.addActionListener(helper);
      helpButton.addActionListener(helper);
      helpItemTOC.addActionListener(helper);

      // assign map IDs for field-level context-sensitive help
      CSH.setHelpIDString(inputField, "text");
      CSH.setHelpIDString(fontChoice, "font");
      CSH.setHelpIDString(boldBox, "bold");
      CSH.setHelpIDString(italicBox, "italic");
      CSH.setHelpIDString(showButton, "view");
      CSH.setHelpIDString(clearButton, "clear");
      CSH.setHelpIDString(helpButton, "help");
      CSH.setHelpIDString(qButton, "whats_this");
      CSH.setHelpIDString(displayField, "text_display");
      CSH.setHelpIDString(foreChoice, "fore_color");
      CSH.setHelpIDString(backChoice, "back_color");

  }

  public static void main(String args[]) {
    (new TypeFacer()).setVisible(true);
  }
}
```

Glossary

Configuration file

A text file with instructions that tell JavaHelp's indexer how to customize the word-search index. You use the configuration file when running the `jhindexer` command so that the information specified in the configuration file is applied to the word-search database as it is created.

Context-sensitive help

Online help that displays a help topic specific to the active function of the software application or situation under which the application is running. Context-sensitive help can be in the form of an online help system opening to a specific help topic, or it can be a feature that displays a brief explanation for a selected control in the application window (known as What's This or *field-level* help).

DTD (Document Type Definition)

A file that contains the rules for the valid syntax, format, and structure for defining the markup elements in an XML document. JavaHelp has DTDs to specify how to process JavaHelp XML files.

Embedded help

Online help that is built into the software application's interface. With embedded help, the user does not have to activate the online help system; it is already displayed with the application's interface. Embedded help does not necessarily have to be in the form of an online help system (although embedded help with JavaHelp is in this form). It can be any help that is embedded in the interface, such as tips and descriptive icons.

Field-level help

Context-sensitive help in which the system displays a brief explanation for a selected object in the application window. Usually users access a special cursor and then click on the object for which they want help. The system then displays a description of that particular object.

HelpSet

All of the files that make up a particular online help document. These files include the HelpSet file, map file(s), navigational files, and help topic files.

HelpSet file

The main HelpSet file that contains all the basic information about the Java-Help system, such as the map file and the navigational components that the JavaHelp system uses. When users access a JavaHelp system, the system first reads the HelpSet file to know what to display in the viewer.

HelpSet Viewer

A special viewer designed specifically for displaying JavaHelp files. It is the main viewer in which JavaHelp systems are displayed.

HTML-based help

Online help systems that use HTML as the source. HTML-based help can be read on all major computer operating systems. Two examples of HTML-based help are Sun Microsystems' JavaHelp and Microsoft's HTML Help.

JAR (Java Archive) file

A compressed file containing one or more Java files. JAR files are based on the popular ZIP files. You can use JAR files for your JavaHelp system to make the system smaller and to organize all the files into one compressed file.

JavaHelp

An online help system from Sun Microsystems. JavaHelp is used primarily with Java applications and applets but can also be used with non-Java programs or as a standalone online documentation system.

JFC (Java Foundation Class)

A set of graphical user interface (GUI) components that design Java applications and applets.

Jhindexer (JavaHelp indexer)

A command to build a word-search index for a JavaHelp system.

JRE (Java Runtime Environment)

A software environment under which Java applications can run. Sun Microsystems' availability of JREs for different computer platforms enables Java applications (such as JavaHelp) to be platform-independent.

Map file

A HelpSet file that contains a list of topic IDs (shorthand names for each topic) along with the associated topic's uniform resource locator (URL). The HelpSet file and navigation files use the map file to know the URL of a topic when they refer to that topic's ID.

Metadata files

Files that contain basic information about the JavaHelp system. These files include the HelpSet file and map file.

Navigation files

Files that contain navigational information about the JavaHelp system. These files include the TOC, index, and word-search index files.

Pop-up window

A small window you can set to display when the user clicks a link in the Java-Help system. You typically use a pop-up window to define a word within a help topic or to provide expanded information for a procedure. See also *secondary window*.

Secondary window

A window you can set to display when the user clicks a link in the JavaHelp system. You typically use a secondary window to provide longer and more detailed information to supplement the information in the original help topic. See also *pop-up window*.

Stopword

A word that is excluded from the word-search index. The purpose of stopwords is to eliminate the redundancy of smaller, more common words, such as "a" or "the," in the word-search index's list of hits.

Topic ID

A shorthand name for a help topic. The JavaHelp system uses topic IDs to simplify working with the HelpSet files. The map file contains a list of every topic URL along with a shorter topic ID. All other files refer to the topic IDs listed in the map file instead of using the longer topic URL. If the JavaHelp author changes the physical URL location for a topic file, he or she needs to update only the location in the map file and not in all of the other HelpSet files.

Topic title

The name, or title, of a help topic. Wording for a topic title is important because users see the topic title in the TOC and word-search index and from this title, decide whether or not to open the help topic.

Tripane window

A display where the window shows three basic sections called panes. The HelpSet Viewer uses a tripane window to provide sections for the menu and toolbar, navigational components, and help topics.

URL (Uniform Resource Locator)

The address on the Internet for a web document. A JavaHelp map file assigns a topic ID to the URL of each help topic, so you don't have to refer to the URL every time you want to link to the help-topic HTML file.

WinHelp

An older and more familiar online help system from Microsoft, designed to support Windows-based applications.

XML (Extensible Markup Language)

A web standard, similar to HTML in structure, that provides a strict set of rules for describing the meaning of data. The HelpSet, map, TOC, and index files are all based on XML.

Index

About the Author

Kevin Lewis (*http://www.kevinlewis.com*) holds a master's degree in technical and professional writing from Northeastern University in Boston. He has worked extensively with many online help systems and was one of the first help authors to work with JavaHelp. He offers training services in several online help technologies. Kevin has published articles on message-box design and on version-control systems for technical documents.

Colophon

Our look is the result of reader comments, our own experimentation, and feedback from distribution channels. Distinctive covers complement our distinctive approach to technical topics, breathing personality and life into potentially dry subjects.

Mary Anne Weeks Mayo was the production editor and copyeditor for *Creating Effective JavaHelp™*. Nicole Arigo and Jane Ellin performed quality control reviews. Emily Quill proofread the book. Anna Snow provided production support. Ellen Troutman-Zaig wrote the index.

Hanna Dyer designed the cover of this book, based on a series design by Edie Freedman. The image of the flashlight was photographed by Kevin Thomas and manipulated in Adobe Photoshop by Michael Snow. The cover layout was produced by Emma Colby using QuarkXPress 4.1, the Bodoni Black font from URW Software, and BT Bodoni Bold Italic from Bitstream. The inside layout was designed by Alicia Cech and David Futato.

Text was produced in FrameMaker 5.5.6 using a template implemented by Mike Sierra. The heading font is Bodoni BT; the text font is New Baskerville. The illustrations that appear in the book were created in Macromedia Freehand 8 and Adobe Photoshop 5 by Robert Romano and Rhon Porter.

 # *More Titles from O'Reilly*

In a Nutshell Quick References

Java Enterprise in a Nutshell

By David Flanagan, Jim Farley,
William Crawford & Kris Magnusson
1st Edition September 1999
622 pages, ISBN 1-56592-483-5

The Java Enterprise APIs are essential building
blocks for creating enterprise-wide distributed
applications in Java. *Java Enterprise in a
Nutshell* covers the RMI, Java IDL, JDBC, JNDI,
Java Servlet, and Enterprise JavaBeans APIs,
providing a fast-paced tutorial and compact reference material on
each of the technologies. Covers Java 2.

Jini in a Nutshell

By Scott Oaks & Henry Wong
1st Edition March 2000
416 pages, ISBN 1-56592-759-1

Jini is a simple set of Java classes and
services that allows devices (i.e., printers)
and services (i.e., printing) to seamlessly
interact with each other. *Jini in a Nutshell*
is an O'Reilly-style quick reference guide to
developing these services and clients using
Jini. It covers everything an experienced Java programmer needs
to know about Jini, including tutorial chapters to get you up to
speed quickly and reference chapters that analyze and explain
every Java package related to Jini.

Java Examples in a Nutshell, 2nd Edition

By David Flanagan
2nd Edition October 2000 (est.)
500 pages (est.), ISBN 0-596-00039-1

In *Java Examples in a Nutshell*, the author
of *Java in a Nutshell* has created an entire
book of example programs that not only
serve as great learning tools, but can also
be modified for individual use. The second
edition of this bestselling book covers
Java 1.3, and includes new chapters on JSP and servlets, XML,
Swing, and Java 2D. This is the book for those who learn best
"by example."

Java in a Nutshell, 3rd Edition

By David Flanagan
3rd Edition November 1999
668 pages, ISBN 1-56592-487-8

The third edition of this bestselling book
covers Java 1.2 and 1.3. It contains an
advanced introduction to Java and its key APIs
and provides quick-reference material on all
the classes and interfaces in the following
APIs: java.lang, java.io, java.beans, java.math,
java.net, java.security, java.text, java.util, and javax.crypto.

Java Foundation Classes in a Nutshell

By David Flanagan
1st Edition September 1999
748 pages, ISBN 1-56592-488-6

Java Foundation Classes in a Nutshell
provides an in-depth overview of the
important pieces of the (JFC), such as
the Swing components and Java 2D. It also
includes compact reference material on all
the GUI- and graphics-related classes in the
numerous javax.swing and java.awt packages. Covers Java 2.

Java

The Java Enterprise CD Bookshelf

By O'Reilly & Associates, Inc.
1st Edition November 2000 (est.)
622 pages (est.), Features CD-ROM
ISBN 1-56592-850-4

The Java Enterprise CD Bookshelf contains
a powerhouse of books from O'Reilly:
both electronic and print versions of *Java
Enterprise in a Nutshell*, plus electronic
versions of *Java in a Nutshell, 3rd Edition*; *Java Foundation
Classes in a Nutshell*; *Enterprise JavaBeans, 2nd Edition*;
Java Servlet Programming; *Java Security*; and *Java Distributed
Computing*.

Java

Java Servlet Programming

By Jason Hunter with William Crawford
1st Edition November 1998
528 pages, ISBN 1-56592-391-X

Java servlets offer a fast, powerful, portable replacement for CGI scripts. *Java Servlet Programming* covers everything you need to know to write effective servlets. Topics include: serving dynamic Web content, maintaining state information, session tracking, database connectivity using JDBC, and applet-servlet communication.

JavaServer Pages

By Hans Bergsten
1st Edition November 2000 (est.)
450 pages (est.), ISBN 1-56592-746-X

JavaServer Pages shows how to develop Java-based web applications without having to be a hardcore programmer. The author provides an overview of JSP concepts and illuminates how JSP fits into the larger picture of web applications. There are chapters for web authors on generating dynamic content, handling session information, and accessing databases, as well as material for Java programmers on creating Java components and custom JSP tags for web authors to use in JSP pages.

Java and XML

By Brett McLaughlin
1st Edition June 2000
498 pages, ISBN 0-596-00016-2

Java revolutionized the programming world by providing a platform-independent programming language. XML takes the revolution a step further with platform-independent language for interchanging data. *Java and XML* shows how to put the two together, building real-world applications in which both the code and the data are truly portable.

Enterprise JavaBeans, 2nd Edition

By Richard Monson-Haefel
2nd Edition March 2000
492 pages, ISBN 1-56592-869-5

Enterprise JavaBeans, 2nd Edition provides a thorough introduction to EJB 1.1 and 1.0 for the enterprise software developer. It shows you how to develop enterprise Beans to model your business objects and processes. The EJB architecture provides a highly flexible system in which components can easily be reused, and which can be changed to suit your needs without upsetting other parts of the system. *Enterprise JavaBeans* teaches you how to take advantage of the flexibility and simplicity that this powerful new architecture provides.

Developing Java Beans

By Robert Englander
1st Edition June 1997
316 pages, ISBN 1-56592-289-1

Developing Java Beans is a complete introduction to Java's component architecture. It describes how to write Beans, which are software components that can be used in visual programming environments. This book discusses event adapters, serialization, introspection, property editors, and customizers, and shows how to use Beans within ActiveX controls.

O'REILLY®

TO ORDER: **800-998-9938** • *order@oreilly.com* • *http://www.oreilly.com/*
OUR PRODUCTS ARE AVAILABLE AT A BOOKSTORE OR SOFTWARE STORE NEAR YOU.
FOR INFORMATION: **800-998-9938** • 707-829-0515 • *info@oreilly.com*

How to stay in touch with O'Reilly

1. Visit Our Award-Winning Web Site

http://www.oreilly.com/

★ "Top 100 Sites on the Web" —*PC Magazine*
★ "Top 5% Web sites" —*Point Communications*
★ "3-Star site" —*The McKinley Group*

Our web site contains a library of comprehensive product information (including book excerpts and tables of contents), downloadable software, background articles, interviews with technology leaders, links to relevant sites, book cover art, and more. File us in your Bookmarks or Hotlist!

2. Join Our Email Mailing Lists

New Product Releases

To receive automatic email with brief descriptions of all new O'Reilly products as they are released, send email to:
listproc@online.oreilly.com
Put the following information in the first line of your message (*not* in the Subject field):
subscribe oreilly-news

O'Reilly Events

If you'd also like us to send information about trade show events, special promotions, and other O'Reilly events, send email to:
listproc@online.oreilly.com
Put the following information in the first line of your message (*not* in the Subject field):
subscribe oreilly-events

3. Get Examples from Our Books via FTP

There are two ways to access an archive of example files from our books:

Regular FTP

- ftp to:
  ftp.oreilly.com
  (login: anonymous
  password: your email address)
- Point your web browser to:
  ftp://ftp.oreilly.com/

FTPMAIL

- Send an email message to:
  ftpmail@online.oreilly.com
  (Write "help" in the message body)

4. Contact Us via Email

order@oreilly.com
To place a book or software order online. Good for North American and international customers.

subscriptions@oreilly.com
To place an order for any of our newsletters or periodicals.

books@oreilly.com
General questions about any of our books.

software@oreilly.com
For general questions and product information about our software. Check out O'Reilly Software Online at **http://software.oreilly.com/** for software and technical support information. Registered O'Reilly software users send your questions to: **website-support@oreilly.com**

cs@oreilly.com
For answers to problems regarding your order or our products.

booktech@oreilly.com
For book content technical questions or corrections.

proposals@oreilly.com
To submit new book or software proposals to our editors and product managers.

international@oreilly.com
For information about our international distributors or translation queries. For a list of our distributors outside of North America check out:
http://www.oreilly.com/www/order/country.html

5. Work with Us

Check out our website for current employment opportunites:
www.jobs@oreilly.com
Click on "Work with Us"

O'Reilly & Associates, Inc.
101 Morris Street, Sebastopol, CA 95472 USA
TEL   707-829-0515 or 800-998-9938
        (6am to 5pm PST)
FAX   707-829-0104

International Distributors

UK, EUROPE, MIDDLE EAST AND AFRICA (EXCEPT FRANCE, GERMANY, AUSTRIA, SWITZERLAND, LUXEMBOURG, LIECHTENSTEIN, AND EASTERN EUROPE)

INQUIRIES
O'Reilly UK Limited
4 Castle Street
Farnham
Surrey, GU9 7HS
United Kingdom
Telephone: 44-1252-711776
Fax: 44-1252-734211
Email: information@oreilly.co.uk

ORDERS
Wiley Distribution Services Ltd.
1 Oldlands Way
Bognor Regis
West Sussex PO22 9SA
United Kingdom
Telephone: 44-1243-779777
Fax: 44-1243-820250
Email: cs-books@wiley.co.uk

FRANCE

INQUIRIES
Éditions O'Reilly
18 rue Séguier
75006 Paris, France
Tel: 33-1-40-51-52-30
Fax: 33-1-40-51-52-31
Email: france@editions-oreilly.fr

ORDERS
GEODIF
61, Bd Saint-Germain
75240 Paris Cedex 05, France
Tel: 33-1-44-41-46-16 (French books)
Tel: 33-1-44-41-11-87 (English books)
Fax: 33-1-44-41-11-44
Email: distribution@eyrolles.com

GERMANY, SWITZERLAND, AUSTRIA, EASTERN EUROPE, LUXEMBOURG, AND LIECHTENSTEIN

INQUIRIES & ORDERS
O'Reilly Verlag
Balthasarstr. 81
D-50670 Köln
Germany
Telephone: 49-221-973160-91
Fax: 49-221-973160-8
Email: anfragen@oreilly.de (inquiries)
Email: order@oreilly.de (orders)

CANADA (FRENCH LANGUAGE BOOKS)

Les Éditions Flammarion ltée
375, Avenue Laurier Ouest
Montréal (Québec) H2V 2K3
Tel: 00-1-514-277-8807
Fax: 00-1-514-278-2085
Email: info@flammarion.qc.ca

HONG KONG

City Discount Subscription Service, Ltd.
Unit D, 3rd Floor, Yan's Tower
27 Wong Chuk Hang Road
Aberdeen, Hong Kong
Tel: 852-2580-3539
Fax: 852-2580-6463
Email: citydis@ppn.com.hk

KOREA

Hanbit Media, Inc.
Chungmu Bldg. 201
Yonnam-dong 568-33
Mapo-gu
Seoul, Korea
Tel: 822-325-0397
Fax: 822-325-9697
Email: hant93@chollian.dacom.co.kr

PHILIPPINES

Global Publishing
G/F Benavides Garden
1186 Benavides Street
Manila, Philippines
Tel: 632-254-8949/637-252-2582
Fax: 632-734-5060/632-252-2733
Email: globalp@pacific.net.ph

TAIWAN

O'Reilly Taiwan
No. 3, Lane 131
Hang-Chow South Road
Section 1, Taipei, Taiwan
Tel: 886-2-23968990
Fax: 886-2-23968916
Email: taiwan@oreilly.com

CHINA

O'Reilly Beijing
Room 2410
160, FuXingMenNeiDaJie
XiCheng District
Beijing, China PR 100031
Tel: 86-10-66412305
Fax: 86-10-86631007
Email: beijing@oreilly.com

INDIA

Computer Bookshop (India) Pvt. Ltd.
190 Dr. D.N. Road, Fort
Bombay 400 001 India
Tel: 91-22-207-0989
Fax: 91-22-262-3551
Email: cbsbom@giasbm01.vsnl.net.in

JAPAN

O'Reilly Japan, Inc.
Yotsuya Y's Building
7 Banch 6, Honshio-cho
Shinjuku-ku
Tokyo 160-0003 Japan
Tel: 81-3-3356-5227
Fax: 81-3-3356-5261
Email: japan@oreilly.com

ALL OTHER ASIAN COUNTRIES

O'Reilly & Associates, Inc.
101 Morris Street
Sebastopol, CA 95472 USA
Tel: 707-829-0515
Fax: 707-829-0104
Email: order@oreilly.com

AUSTRALIA

Woodslane Pty., Ltd.
7/5 Vuko Place
Warriewood NSW 2102
Australia
Tel: 61-2-9970-5111
Fax: 61-2-9970-5002
Email: info@woodslane.com.au

NEW ZEALAND

Woodslane New Zealand, Ltd.
21 Cooks Street (P.O. Box 575)
Waganui, New Zealand
Tel: 64-6-347-6543
Fax: 64-6-345-4840
Email: info@woodslane.com.au

LATIN AMERICA

McGraw-Hill Interamericana
Editores, S.A. de C.V.
Cedro No. 512
Col. Atlampa
06450, Mexico, D.F.
Tel: 52-5-547-6777
Fax: 52-5-547-3336
Email: mcgraw-hill@infosel.net.mx

O'REILLY®

O'REILLY WOULD LIKE TO HEAR FROM YOU

Which book did this card come from?

_____

Where did you buy this book?
- ❏ Bookstore
- ❏ Direct from O'Reilly
- ❏ Bundled with hardware/software
- ❏ Computer Store
- ❏ Class/seminar
- ❏ Other _____

What operating system do you use?
- ❏ UNIX
- ❏ Windows NT
- ❏ Macintosh
- ❏ PC(Windows/DOS)
- ❏ Other _____

What is your job description?
- ❏ System Administrator
- ❏ Network Administrator
- ❏ Web Developer
- ❏ Programmer
- ❏ Educator/Teacher
- ❏ Other _____

❏ Please send me O'Reilly's catalog, containing a complete listing of O'Reilly books and software.

Name _____ Company/Organization _____

Address _____

City _____ State _____ Zip/Postal Code _____ Country _____

Telephone _____ Internet or other email address (specify network) _____

Nineteenth century wood engraving
of a bear from the O'Reilly &
Associates Nutshell Handbook®
Using & Managing UUCP.

BUSINESS REPLY MAIL

FIRST CLASS MAIL   PERMIT NO. 80   SEBASTOPOL, CA

Postage will be paid by addressee

O'Reilly & Associates, Inc.
101 Morris Street
Sebastopol, CA 95472-9902